AROUND AND ABOUT THE FAL

David Mudd

BOSSINEY BOOKS

First published in 1989 by
Bossiney Books
St Teath, Bodmin, Cornwall.

Typeset and Printed by
Clowes Book Printers
St Columb, Cornwall.

Bound by R Booth (Bookbinders) Ltd
Mabe Burnthouse, Cornwall

Front cover photography – Royal Institution
of Cornwall

Back cover photography – The National Trust

PLATE ACKNOWLEDGMENTS
David and Diana Mudd: pages 3, 4, 5, 6, 9, 10,
18, 19, 20, 21, 24, 25, 27, 29, 33, 35, 36, 44, 45,
46, 52, 54, 55, 57, 59, 63, 75, 76, 78, 79, 80, 81,
82, 83, 84, 85, 86, 87, 88, 90, 92, 93, 96, 98, 99,
102

Royal Institution of Cornwall: pages 8, 13, 14,
15, 51, 66, 67, 70, 72, 74, 95, 101

The National Trust: pages 12, 41, 42

Royal Cornwall Polytechnic Society: pages 16,
66, 67, 89, 100

Sylvia and Stewart Hood: pages 50, 51, 53

Wheal Martyn Museum: pages 91, 94

About the Author and the Book

David Mudd

There's nothing new in a portrait of the River Fal – artists, writers, poets and geographers have been hard at work for at least the last two thousand years, as records since those of Ptolemy would seem to show.

But the real picture of the Fal is painted as much in the deeds of its inhabitants; the grandeur of its great houses; and the stories of its communities through the ages as it is in prose, in poem or in artist's colours.

In *Around and About the Fal,* David Mudd has drawn from more than two dozen different sources to create a broad and rich tapestry of a river and its people; its industries and interests; its prosperity and past.

He introduces us to heroes, to wrongdoers, to men of vision, men of valour and men of veneration; to saints and sinners; to those who would buy or sell a wife as freely as a horse; to writers and clerics; to the foolish and the forthright. He takes us through picturesque lanes to villages with romantic names; and to former great river ports where the ships and great waters are now but a memory.

In this, his eleventh complete book and fourth co-title for Bossiney Books, he is joined by the talents of his wife, Diana, who is responsible for many of the photographs of the river and its churches and communities as they are today.

'The book was a natural for us, not a chore', David says. 'We fell deeply in love with the Fal a few years ago when, during a period afloat on the boat I then owned, we made our way secretly at dusk to a perfect mooring we had discovered off Tregothnan at a place we called Mud Creek. No sooner had we cut the engines, opened the wine and started a belated meal than the river took on a character of its own. Downstream, at King Harry passage, methane tankers rode at anchor. Over at Tolverne the late evening became alive with the sounds and smells of those enjoying a barbecue while, just away from Mud Creek, a floating disco glided by with its lights a-dancing and its passengers a-jigging.

'As the river settled down to peace, fish jumped around us; swans drifted down into the golden path of the young moon. As I cannot use paintbox and brush, I decided that the only way of capturing the magic of this most majestic and beautiful of rivers would be through words. Not my words, but the words of those who have witnessed the Fal in all its moods from a hundred different points of view and experiences in the four hundred years or so since men first committed reliable reports and descriptions to paper.'

The Fal is, he says, a waterway of magic, of mystery and of spectacle – but, above all, of colour and of great charm. In *Around and About the Fal,* he has not tried to tell everything ... but more to provide an appetiser that will attract many to share this unique historic and scenic delight.

'And those who are attracted will find more', he says. 'But, above all, they will find a charm and a character to which they will become addicted.'

Born in Falmouth, in 1933, David Mudd has many qualifications for having written *Around and About the Fal.* From a seafaring family – and as a former Merchant Navy officer himself – he has always had a love and respect for what he regards as his local river. As a former journalist on local newspapers, and as a BBC and ITV reporter, he has reflected the romance and the tradition of the district in print and in prose. As Member of Parliament for Falmouth and Camborne since 1970, he has represented the interests of many modern-time residents who live on, beside or near the river's enchanted waters.

Diana Mudd

5

A RIVER OF CONSEQUENCE
AND BEAUTY

CAN any river challenge its beauty, its birds, its shameless contradiction of bustle and leisure, its creek-side communities, its charm and its history? Or is the River Fal unique?

If not unique, then few would deny that it has a magic and an atmospheric character that make it a living phenomenon rather than just another pretty waterway . . . and even fewer would argue against Arthur Mee's belief that it provides ' one of the loveliest river-crossings in all England', or that of Claude Berry that it is, perhaps, 'the most enchanting of South Cornwall's deep and bosky river valleys'.

Never come across 'bosky'? Well, it means bushy or wooded. And the Fal lives up to that description in that the wide variety of trees

Cowlands Creek

'The deep and bosky Fal.'

and bushes that flank the river appear to grow from beneath those deep sparkling waters, or sprout from overhanging banks rather than pushing their way skywards from the safety of the shore itself.

But the Fal is more than trees. It's a living feast of bird-life where herons stand motionless, kingfishers can be seen, and where – as swans carry out their endless progress through the water in a rhythmic poem of effortless motion – the woodpecker busily carries out the task from which he takes his name. Squirrels scamper in the trees and, as if contradicting the laws of nature, actually enter the water to swim with the confidence and the agility of water animals. The rich golden brown of autumn bracken is studded by the golder tones of a fox going about his patrol, or by the vivid reds, blues and browns of a cock pheasant.

There's even poetry in the names of the Fal's settlements – Cowlands and Coombe; Creed and Lamorran; Golden Mill and Ruan. The crops, for from Fal to Tamar is known as Cornwall's rich granary, are joined by the soft flesh and rich tasty juices of plums. In addition to a wide variety of fish that seem to defy the fisherman to catch them, there are oysters.

7

Cowlands Creek around 1880.

Tregothnan atop the Fal –
1907.

Oysters were probably brought by the Romans, for the Fal was certainly an important trading river long before the days of Julius Caesar, with merchants wishing to buy the rich minerals which came to the surface in the upper-reaches but which then, sadly, strangled that which they had created as their sands silted-up the head of the river and forced access slowly but constantly downstream.

In addition to its role as a maritime waterway, the Fal now provides a setting for unbelievable contrasts where tiny yachts and dinghies are dwarfed by huge ships at anchor and whose stillness and patience seem to add to the urgency of the tiny man-filled minnows that race past them in a size reversed that resembles the minute birds that bustle around the stationary rhinoceros.

It is easy to get confused as to where you are. The boatman talks of a 'River Fal trip', but takes you down from Truro and past Malpas on the way – although this part of the journey is but a tiny fraction of the intricate tracery of streams and rivers that give the Fal its name.

There are the Truro River, the Tresillian River and the Ruan River to name but a few. Indeed, it is difficult to trace just where the Fal begins in that complex and barren area known as the Goss Moor in the spine of Cornwall.

The waters merge together near Tregothnan, then nurture, nourish and nudge a shoreline of unbroken beauty extending into a

Almost too good to be true – Cowlands Creek in 1989 and still little changed.

Coombe Creek.

dozen inlets before, by Mylor and St Just they come together in that vast meeting point known as Carrick Roads before sweeping out to the sea between St Mawes and Falmouth.

Indeed, even its name distinguishes it as being a river of consequence. Its tributaries are marked with their name first, and 'river' second. But the Fal is the *River Fal*, due to a decision taken by Ordnance Survey, as Britain's official map-makers, in 1906 on the advice of the then Lord Falmouth.

In Great Britain, except in the case of certain administrative names, there is no national body or group of bodies that has the responsibility for laying down, for official use, the names and spellings of places appearing on official maps or in other formal documents.

Ordnance Survey therefore took on the role of deciding what names would appear, how they should be spelt, and where they should be placed on the map. In reaching this difficult decision, it was guided mainly by local opinion, custom and belief.

Thus, for years many Cornish rivers had the word 'river' after the place with which they were associated. However, in 1906, Mr Julian Hill, principal agent to Lord Falmouth, requested that from that date onwards the river should be known as the River Fal.

Certainly early maps and descriptions were very confusing indeed.

One dated 1579 sketched its course accurately but described it as *Vale Flud*. This would appear to go back to a document dated AD 969 and which referred to *Faele*, although the river was probably known before *Tregny, Grampound, Crede* and *St Steven* were recorded.

In 1584, John Norden produced the first maps of Britain showing roads accurately and with the counties drawn to scale. Even more important, he described the towns he included in his maps.

Writing of the river *Vale* 'that falleth by *Tregny*', he spoke of the silting-up that was already taking place and would, 300 years later, be attracting a suggested levy of 1/2d per ton on output to cover the costs of dredging.

'In this our Cornwall the sea in former tymes hath yielded great kindenes, to bring boates of reasonable burden far aboue *Tregny*; but the sea hauing refused this office of ease to that parte of the Country, checked (as it seemeth) by the minerall sandes which fall into manie places, to the preiudice of the hauens.'

Tregny, or *Tregeny*, he described as: 'a market towne and an incorporation . . . which is a verie poore town graced sometymes with *Pomery* castle, the ruynes whereof yet speake, as thet lye altogether rent on the topp of a mounte'.

Of Grampound, or *Gromponde*, Norden wrote: 'a borrowe towne, and a pryuiledged market, but of small resorte; the towne is verye Auntient, the pryuildges large, the inhanitants few and poore'.

St Stephen, or *St Steuens*, consisted of: 'A church standinge amonge the moarishe hills'.

'An intricate tracery of streams' – 1912.

The next pictorial record came in the early 1600s when John Speed recorded the *Valle Flud* going beyond *Sct Stephens* to a point near Roche, with settlements at *Grompint, Creed, Tregnye, Trevithen* and *Tregunnon*.

Interestingly, long after Falmouth had received its Royal Charter recognising the town, geographically at least, as being at the mouth of the Fal, Richard Blome's map of 1715 refers to *Vale flu* as the river, but Falmouth as the town! Only in the 1780s did the River Fal appear on a map in its present name and following its present course.

By then the most southerly – and beautiful – church looking over the estuary of the Fal was a mere 500 years old. Built in 1256, the little church of St Just-in-Roseland was recreated only five years later and then further reconstructed in the 1400s.

Quaint, diminutive and attractive 'though the church may be with its carved bench-ends, its rood stairs and roof carvings, and its five-hundred year-old font, much of its appeal lies in its sub-tropical setting, providing ferns, flowers and shrubs in unbelievable profusion.

The entrance is so steep that from the road it looks as if the

Trelissick looks down to the Fal – 1912.

lychgate is on the same level as the tower and sits astride a vibrant display of Chilean myrtle, fire bush, palms, fuchsias and magnolia.

To visit St Just in spring or summer, when the church is bathed in sunshine and the churchyard seems to simmer in the heat, may give a false belief that temperatures never fall and that frost and ice never make their numbing presence felt.

But they do.

In October 1887, for instance, there was a public outcry about the failure of the authorities to buy sufficient coal to keep the school warm, it being said that: 'The children sit trembling with the cold for several hours daily. The school being built upon the top of a hill, and the school being too small for the duties thereof, necessitates one part of its duties being performed in the porch, and the condition of the children is thus rendered dreadfully disagreeable, and, indeed, dangerous to health'.

But the Fal is the river of ferries.

Records dating back to 1468 refer to one across Devoran Creek from Restronguet to the Feock side. Long before the main road was built it formed an important crossing on the post-road from Falmouth to Truro.

In 1664 the ferry business at Tolverne, linking Roseland with Truro, was let as part of an enterprise which, in addition to the ferry, included the boat and the fares, half the fish caught at Tolverne Weir, the ferryman's house and cellars, three fields, the right to land sand and to dry nets, to pasture two horses, to draw fresh water from a spring, and to gather furze, thorns and broom for fuel. The rent was set at a yearly figure of 26s 8d (£1.33).

Then there was the ferry that ran between Tregothnan and Malpas. Malpas, it was said, came from the French 'mal-pas', meaning

King Harry Ferry in 1910. A very different looking method of transport to that of today although chains still move the ferry from one bank to the other as they clearly did in this old photograph.

13

'The most romantic of all passages' – Malpas in 1902 when the
ferry was a vital link across the river.

King Harry Ferry in the 1880s
and a very basic method of
crossing the river. Note the
planks for getting the trap off
the boat.

'a bad passage'. It was claimed that it was used by Queen Iseult on her way to meet King Mark and is said to be 'the most romantic of all passages in Britain. It is also one of the most beautiful'.

In 1674, it was let at an annual rental of £1, the lease to cover the ferry houses on either side of the crossing as well as the ferryboat. In a life spanning two centuries, Jane Davies was the ferryman at Malpas from 1770 to 1832 when she died at the age of 82. She was known as 'Mopus Jenny', the 'Mopus' coming from the local way of pronouncing 'Malpas'.

But to tourist, motorist, 'local' and travel-historian alike, the best-known ferry across the Fal **is** that which carries traffic across King Harry Passage and safely over the deepest points of the river.

Many believe that it takes its name from a connection with King Henry VIII and who, having used it, gave both passage and ferry the use of his name. It's a fascinating thought, but one that is wrong by a couple of Henrys and several decades as the Henry in question was undoubtedly Henry VI, a gentle, loving and pleasant monarch, rather than his flashy, blustering – but more famous – Tudor namesake.

In documents dating back to 1566 and 1585, the passage is

Another King Harry Ferry – chain driven but already beginning to take the shape of the present day ferry. This ferry was operating in 1920.

Ships laid up in the River Fal near Tolverne after the 1914-18 war. The river here is extremely deep and is still a popular anchorage for ships awaiting re-fits or work.

recorded as 'Kybyllys' of 'Kebellyes', words that seem to have an uncanny link with the Welsh word for a ferry-boat, 'ceubal'.

In those years the rental for the right to run a ferry stood at 6d (2¹/2p) a year. In 1649, so H L Douch recalls in *Old Cornish Inns,* one John Taylor wrote: 'that day I passed a ferry called King Harry's Passage (but why it is so named few men know) there I lodged at the ferryman's house'.

Leslie Douch says that the passage took its name from the chapel dedicated to 'Our Lady and King Henry VI' on the Tolverne side.

Certainly the ferry had a long and interesting life, being used for soldiers, horses and stores at the time of the Civil War, and for animals, fodder, produce and people at other times – often resembling Noah's Ark when loaded with horses, cattle or sheep.

In 1887, *The West Briton* reported: 'During the last 30 years the question has often been discussed privately and publicly whether there could not be a better way of crossing the River Fal at King Harry Ferry than has hitherto existed – a simple ferry-boat, rowed across by one or two men. With a strong south-easterly wind the passage is frequently impassable, and travellers, who have come eight or ten miles hoping to cross the ferry, have been obliged to retrace their steps and go round by Truro and Tregony – a distance of twenty miles (thirty-three kilometres) further than they anticipated. A high level bridge has been suggested by some and a steam ferry by others: but up to the present time no change whatever has been made'.

In fact, change *was* on the way – with steampower triumphing

16

over bridge-building. At the end of 1889 'a wonderful accommodation for the district' was operating – in the form of the new steam ferry. A service every quarter of an hour crossed the river in under four minutes at a charge, for carriages, of 1s. 6d. (7½p). 'A great advantage is that passengers and conveyances can be taken over at any time of tide and in any weather, the former ordinary horse-boat being unable to cross the river when a strong breeze was blowing from the south'.

The tradition of manpower and musclepower may have given way to that of coal and water harnessed in steam, but the romance and picturesque nature of the crossing – with its indescribably beautiful country approach roads on either side – remain unchanged and unthreatened in keeping with the ageless majesty and setting of the river at one of its most captivating and historic points.

An old picture postcard of King Harry Ferry in 1904.

17

ONE MASS OF NOTORIOUS CORRUPTION
The Grampound of Yesteryear

DESPITE many recorded less-than-enthusiastic comments about its appearance by a variety of writers over the years, there is no denying the fact that Grampound *is* grand.

No, not in the accepted sense, but in that its name is a corruption of 'Grand Pont', recalling the Roman bridge that once spanned the River Fal at this point and, some 600 years ago, established Grampound as one of Cornwall's oldest and most successful commercial communities.

It was given a charter in 1332 and was recorded as having a single street running down to the bridge and lying astride the main road from Callington to Truro, Penryn and Helston. Granting the charter, Earl John of Eltham gave the townspeople the rare right of being able to hang convicted thieves in their own town; an exemption from paying tolls and taxes for the repair and building of other bridges; freedom to set up stalls in their own markets without payment of dues; and to hold 52 markets and two fairs every year.

However, Earl John was not all-giving. In fact he found a way of getting a great deal back from the community by ensuring that all corn had to be ground in his mill and by charging royalties on corn so treated. If anyone was caught trying a spot of private enterprise either

'There is no denying the fact that Grampound is grand.' These youngsters were clearly enticed by the prospect of being caught on camera at the turn of the century.

by operating an illegal mill of their own, or by taking their corn elsewhere to avoid payment, there was an instant and heavy fine.

When he visited Grampound, John Wesley found that, in 400 years, prosperity and pride had slumped to an unrecognisable level. In its place was: 'a mean, inconsiderable, dirty village. However, it is a borough town!'

At noon he started preaching to a large congregation in a meadow on the outskirts of the town. While talking he was aware of the ominous figure of a man in black on the far side of the crowd. When the man said: 'Come down, you have no business there', Wesley took it that he was talking to a group of interested youngsters who rapidly abandoned their vantage point on a hedge.

He was wrong.

As he continued with his sermon, the man in black walked away . . . only to return later with two constables and to identify himself as the mayor and minister of the borough. One of the constables walked politely up to Wesley and said: 'Sir, the mayor says you shall not preach within his borough'.

Wesley's narrative goes on: 'I answered "the mayor has no authority to hinder me; but it is a point not worth contesting". So I

'Grampound consists mainly of one street.' And here is that street in 1893.

went about a musket-shot farther, and left the borough to Mr. Mayor's disposal.'

It is possible that John Wesley was aware of the deliberate irony of his remark, since Grampound – in Parliamentary terms – was very much at the mayor's disposal.

In one of the many scandals surrounding the buying and selling of votes, Grampound was to feature prominently. Assessing the elections at Grampound in 1747, Thomas Pitt recorded: 'As for Grampound I think we can carry it, but it must cost damnably dear, the villains rise in their demands so extravagantly that I have been very near damning them and kicking them to the devil at once.' In a later report to the House of Commons, Grampound was described as: 'one mass of notorious corruption; all the electors received money; all received it openly.'

Grampound's seven-sided cross.

In the 1821 elections one of the candidates, Sir Manasseh Lopes, offered 40 of the voting freemen £35 each for their votes. They demanded £50 and were paid in full. For arranging the deal the mayor received 'an acknowledgment' of £300.

In another election, in 1727, the going rate was £20 to each of the 42 voters; £40 each to the three magistrates; and £160 to the mayor, plus £172 for beer, meals, musicians and entertainers for the freemen and the magistrates. Small wonder then, that John Wesley was willing to leave the borough 'to the mayor's disposal'.

In 1831, 10,000 Cornishmen presented a petition demanding the elimination of the system whereby there was no true Parliamentary representation and Cornwall returned 44 Members as against 45 for the whole of Scotland and none at all for many large cities in England and Wales, such as Manchester and Leeds.

The Reform Bill of 1832 cut Cornwall's share of Parliamentary seats to a more representative six, and Grampound's more notorious reputation was laid to rest.

By then, though, things had changed. The mills were quiet, few travellers called, the river was silted and still. One visitor wrote in 1829: 'Once remarkable as having been one of the Borough towns of the county, it principally consists of one street, but the houses have a decayed and mean appearance; it however possesses a tolerable good inn. Nearly in the centre of the town is an antient *Chapel*, in which, till lately, divine service was performed, but now fast mouldering to decay, with a small septangular cross in front of it. The *Market-house* is also a very antique structure. Grampound contains, according to

The toll house at Grampound which many tried to avoid.

late returns, 668 inhabitants, being an increase of only 67 during the last 10 years.'

Certainly the place was running itself down at an alarming rate, although the influence of the church was still strong – a local employer offering a job to someone, stating: 'if a religious character, the more acceptable.'

Hooliganism has a place in the records, too.

One important source of revenue was the toll-gate at the bottom of Grampound Hill. Trying to escape payment by often ingenious means was regarded as good sport.

Fines for evasion were heavy. Persons 'passing through the Grounds to avoid the Turnpike, or Occupiers permitting the same' faced a penalty of £5. The same surcharge was imposed on persons 'turning out of the road, or taking off Horses to avoid payment of the Tolls.' It seems that many waggons arrived in the vicinity of the turnpike pulled by more horses than actually dragged them past the toll-booth, a 'light' horse attracting a lower charge than one actually in the shafts.

Persons 'refusing to pay the tolls or resisting Collectors' were fined £10 for their pains, while the most serious view of all was taken of those caught in the act of actually altering or re-using tickets.

In October 1821 the toll-house was attacked during the night by a person or persons who systematically removed the roof, pulled down the chimney, and threw the actual stop-bar over Grampound bridge. A reward of £10 soon led to the detection of the miscreants.

In 1872, according to *The West Briton*, a deserter from the Army, named May, found work as a miner near Grampound. 'He married and became a resident in the vicinity of the mine, and succeeded in concealing his whereabouts until the early part of last week. On Tuesday an inspector of police, accompanied by two constables, one a crack runner, visited the mine for the purpose of taking him in charge, and finding that he was underground, the inspector sent his men down the mine to apprehend him. Soon afterwards a miner made his appearance at the mouth of the shaft, where stood the inspector who asked him if his name was May. "No, but the police are coming with him". He then quietly walked away until some few hundred yards distant, when he commenced to run ...'

THE WEALTHY, THE BRAVE, THE COMPASSIONATE AND THE CORRUPT
The families and personalities of the Fal

MEN of courage, conviction, books and bribery stud the history of some of the communities of the River Fal and its estuary. Men of wealth, men of stealth, men of knowledge and men of belief.

If the Boscawen family dominated the eighteenth century through the reputation of one man, Edward Boscawen, then it was a logical progression from the late thirteenth century when one of his predecessors, Henry de Boscawen, married Hawise Trewoof and set in motion a long consequential series of marriages that established the Boscawens as the most influential and well-connected family in the Duchy.

They moved to Tregothnan when, soon after 1335, John de Boscawen married Joan de Tregothnan. John's son took as his wife the heiress, Joan de Albalanda, whose family estates were on the opposite

Highly decorative Tregothnan in 1904.

23

Edward Boscawen – 'Old Dreadnought' – who feared nothing but disgrace. He is immortalised in stone in St Michael Penkevil Church.

side of the Fal, at Kea, thus forging a strong presence on both river banks. Later Boscawens married the Tolvernes, the Trewarthenicks, the Tregarricks and the Dangrous of Carclew, thus strengthening their landowning hold on the Fal.

Wider afield, in Cornish terms, Boscawens became intertwined in a series of marriages with Arundells, the Bassetts, the St Aubyns, the Lowers, the Godolphins, the Carminows, the Trenoweths and the Trevanions, as if to underline the undeniable Cornishness of their line.

Early Boscawens, for some reason best known to themselves, did not relish having honours bestowed upon them – perhaps because going to London to carry out Court duties was too much of a chore.

An old engraving of Tregothnan as it looked in 1831.

Certainly Richard Boscawen preferred to pay a penalty of £5 rather than attend the coronation of Henry VII and being made a knight of the Bath. As if to prove that this was a family tradition, his grandson, Hugh, repeated paying the fine and giving the 'thumbs down' to the Bath when Queen Mary was crowned.

Although the early Boscawens were rather self-effacing in national terms, and were not interested in advancement, the first exception came in the shape of Hugh – the grandson of the one who risked offending Queen Mary – and who became Recorder of Truro and was knighted in 1626, having held the quaint title of Chief of the Coat Armour during an official visitation to Cornwall in 1620.

He had at least two sons, Edward and Hugh.

Edward represented Truro in Parliament throughout the reign of King Charles II; married one of the Godolphins; and sired yet another Hugh who, in 1720, was to become the first Baron Boscawen and Viscount Falmouth.

Edward's brother, Nicholas Boscawen, joined the Parliamentary army during the Civil War but died when he was only 22 years old. So respected had the family become that he was buried, for a time, in Westminster Abbey. However, at the time of the Restoration, his body was dug up and unceremoniously thrown into a common grave in the nearby St Margaret's churchyard.

Hugh Boscawen, first Baron Boscawen and Viscount Falmouth, was the leading Whig politician in the Cornwall of his day. The Parliamentary representation of both Penryn and Tregony was in his absolute control. Before his promotion to the House of Lords, he was MP for Tregony from 1702-1705; for the County of Cornwall from 1705-1710; for Truro from 1710-1713; and for Penryn from 1713-1720. He spent lavishly to provide voters with 'inducements' to vote for Whig candidates and his elevation was as much in return for this as to pacify his growing indignation and impatience that he had not been ennobled.

He had, however, been allocated a string of colourful and important tasks along the way. He was appointed 'Groom of the Bedchamber' to Prince George of Denmark; Steward of the Duchy of Cornwall; Lord Warden of the Stannaries; Comptroller of the Royal Household; and Joint Vice-Treasurer of Ireland.

Certainly his ambition rubbed off on his wife, a former Charlotte Churchill. So determined was she to become a Lady of the Bedchamber to the wife of King George II that she resorted to bribery to win the post.

Perhaps it was inevitable that Hugh and Charlotte – she was, after all, an ancestor of Winston Churchill and a niece of the Duke of Marlborough – should produce a son who would embody the fusion of the many good points of the respective families in honour, integrity, decisiveness, humanity and courage.

Edward Boscawen, born on August 19, 1711 was to be just such a progeny.

Born at Tregothnan, it was said of him that: 'He feared nothing but disgrace; he was as gentle as a woman in the presence of suffering; he was wise and provident in fighting sickness and privation'.

He joined the Navy as a lad of twelve, learning at first hand the important duty of waging war and the rarer art of winning battles. Lord Chatham wrote of him, when he was still a junior officer: 'When I apply to other officers respecting an expedition, they always raise difficulties. Boscawen always finds expedients.'

He was undoubtedly a resourceful young man. When one of his boats was badly holed by a cannon-ball in a shore skirmish, he horrified seamen used to the unbending tradition of officers and gentlemen, by tearing off his wig and stuffing it in the hole.

In 1726 he was appointed to the 60-gunner, *HMS Superbe*, and sailed to the West Indies under Admiral Hosier. Aboard *Superbe* he met another junior officer, Lieutenant John Byng, whom he was later to meet again under extremely distasteful circumstances.

It is true to say that Midshipman Boscawen and Lieutenant Byng

Trewithen – 'house of election scandals'.

did not hit it off, Boscawen noting in his diary that his superior had a marked consistency when it came to shirking dangerous or unpleasant tasks.

Certainly service on the West Indies station was far from pleasant – especially for a shirker. Yellow fever and vicious land-crabs added to the dangers and the discomforts of the posting. While Boscawen did all he could to help in the near-impossible task of trying to make life tolerable for the men, Byng managed to get a transfer back to Britain.

How great were the health hazards from which Byng fled? In fifteen months, Admiral Hosier's squadron lost 4,000 men including the admiral, eight captains and 50 lieutenants. Moved by the carnage of disease, young Boscawen committed himself that when he obtained a command of his own: 'I shall change the condition of life and service whereby sickness claims more lives of the King's sailors than do enemy cannon.'

At the age of 21, Edward Boscawen was promoted lieutenant and given his first command – *HMS Hector* – in the Mediterranean. He started putting his beliefs into action and insisted on high fitness, high morale and, as far as bad Naval regulations and rations would allow, a proper and balanced diet for his men.

By 1739, Britain was at war with Spain and he distinguished himself in the battle of Porto Bello, winning further honours, two years later, at Cartagene.

Within five years the war encompassed France as well as Spain and Boscawen, already one of the most experienced and respected officers in the Navy, was posted – at the age of 33 – to the ship whose name he would carry for the rest of his life, the 60-gun *HMS Dreadnought*. While cruising in the English Channel, he took the French frigate *Medee*, with 800 of her crew. By a strange coincidence, *Medee* was commanded by Le Comte de Hocquart whom Boscawen would capture in another encounter eleven years hence.

Medee, the first ship to be captured in the war, was sent to England with a prize crew. It was hoped that she could be repaired and refitted and sail with the Royal Navy. But such hopes were in vain as she was found to be below Royal Navy standards and was sold to private owners. Renamed *Boscawen*, she sailed for a further eighteen years before literally falling to bits through old age, poor materials and bad design.

Boscawen's successful and popular first campaign against the French peaked with the battle of Finisterre, on May 3, 1747, when he was severely wounded in the shoulder by a musket-ball. Honoured for his heroism, leadership and strategies, he was promoted to the list of Flag Officers – specially extended by one so that he could be added – and was given the very unusual appointment of Commander-in-Chief of His Majesty's Forces by Sea and Land in the East Indies. Not only was he then England's youngest Commander-in-Chief, but he was the first co-ordinating supreme commander for both Army and Navy for almost a century, having under his command a squadron of six ships of

**Tregothnan in 1842 –
'romantic and castellated.'**

the line, four smaller warships and a back-up of supply and troopships.

His service on the way to the East Indies was impeccable. But, at Pondicherry, he faced his greatest tactical challenge. It involved the evacuation of hundreds of Europeans in danger of massacre.

Boscawen's command consisted of more than 5,000 marines, sailors and soldiers, with another 1,000 Indian troops. In theory the task should have posed few problems. However, the saying 'careless talk costs lives' had not been coined in those days and the enemy, in the shape of the French, with native support, knew he was on the way and had ample time to prepare their own positions against him.

Even worse, from Boscawen's point of view, was that his orders demanded that he should be guided by the skilled knowledge of the engineers on technical points. Having already found engineers to be tactically weak, defensively incompetent, and a supportive liability, he was at an obvious disadvantage. His men had to wait eighteen days while the engineers tried to dismantle an insignificant fort. They had to camp in a remote and inconvenient place thus being tired when action began. The engineers insisted that stores be landed in unwise places and, having little knowledge of the capability of ships' guns,

29

rushed off to dig trenches and tunnels where no covering fire could be provided.

Hit by disease, and with the rainy season closing in, he had to abandon the operation and, with more than 1,000 Europeans dead, take his squadron, raise the siege, and run for Trincomalee.

Recalled to England, he was appointed a Lord Commissioner of the Admiralty and, in 1755, promoted Vice-Admiral, given a squadron, and ordered to sail to North America to destroy a large French naval presence.

With eleven men-o'-war he was despatched with the blunt instruction to sink any French ship he discovered, be it military or civilian. The French gave an official warning that they would regard the discharge of even one British gun as a declaration of war.

Ignoring the threat, 'Old Dreadnought' as he was, by then, known by sailors of all nations, sailed to the waters off Newfoundland where he found a squadron led by his old adversary, Le Comte de Hocquart. In a short skirmish he captured two French ships and 1,500 men.

The other French ships fled to the safety of the St Lawrence river and, as nothing more could be done until they returned to sea, Boscawen took his squadron and men to Nova Scotia in the hope of easing a very dangerous fever that was laying his men down like ninepins. Putting the welfare of his men first, he took it on his own

Tregothnan boathouse and the scene of a family outing in 1910.

initiative to return to England as quickly as he could. The passage was not speedy enough, and the virus so deadly, that 2,000 men perished before they dropped anchor off Spithead.

In the spell in home waters that followed, he was involved in what he probably regarded as a distasteful rather than distressing task as a Lord Commissioner of the Admiralty. It involved his adversary of many years ago, John Byng.

Like Boscawen, Byng had earned rapid promotion and, by 1756, was an Admiral. Given an extremely ill-equipped force, he was sent to raise the French blockade of Minorca. Due to a bad appreciation of the situation and muddled tactics – but certainly not due to the cowardice of which he was later accused – Byng's fleet suffered immense losses and withdrew.

Public opinion was outraged. Having to find a scapegoat, the Admiralty had Byng brought home under arrest and put before a Court Martial charged with cowardice. It fell to Edward Boscawen both to sign the order for the Court Martial and, at its conclusion, to sign the order for immediate execution on the lesser charge of neglect of duty, the cowardice charge having failed.

The Board of Admiralty ordered Boscawen to proceed with the necessary arrangements ' to cause Admiral Byng to be shot to death on board such of His Majesty's ships he shall think proper.'

The sentence was carried out, efficiently, by Byng himself. Spurning the services of a firing-squad commander, the Admiral dropped a white handkerchief when he was ready for execution.

In Boscawen's mind it mattered not that Byng had been cleared of cowardice. Any man, who through bungling incompetence or indecision at a time of crisis cost the lives of his men, endangered his fleet and disgraced His Majesty, deserved death.

Further honours followed and, in 1758 – having been Member of Parliament for Truro (nominally) from 1742-1750 – he was called to the House of Commons for the thanks of Parliament. Next year he became a member of the Privy Council and, a few days later, as commander of a new squadron, put to sea again in the continuing conflict with France.

This time he flew his flag on the 90-gun ship *HMS Namur* and commanded fourteen major warships and two smaller ones. His immediate task was to stop the two halves of the French fleet linking up between Brest and Toulon for a joint invasion of England.

Becoming bored when the French stayed out of harm's way safely in Toulouse, he sent in three ships to attack those of the enemy lying nearest the sea in an attempt to either coax or defy them out to the open sea. Coastal batteries disabled his ships and he had to tow them out and make for Gibraltar for repairs and fresh water and provisions.

No sooner had his squadron reached Gibraltar and stood down but news reached them that the French were making a dash for freedom. Within two-and-a-half hours Boscawen's ships were back at sea and ready for action.

On August 18, 1759, he engaged the enemy. Somehow their fleet had become split in their time at sea and, as he assessed them, he realised that there were only twelve of them in sight. In a short and decisive battle eight were either destroyed or surrendered and the remaining four fled to the neutrality of Portuguese waters.

While being fully aware of neutrality and of the needs and demands to respect it, Boscawen cruised off Lagos Bay calling the French out to finish the fight. When the French refused, he risked an international incident by sailing into Portugal's territorial waters; sinking two enemy warships; and pursuing the other two until they were run aground and scuttled by their captains.

For this he was awarded a pension of £3,000 per year; given the freedom of Edinburgh; the (notional) Parliamentary representation of Bodmin; and appointment to the utmost post of co-ordination of the forces of the Crown, General of Marines.

He died, of fever, in January 1761.

His tomb, in the church of St Michael Penkevil, records: 'His birth tho' noble, his titles tho' illustrious, were but incidental additions to his greatness.

'In his high departments masterly and upright. His example form'd, while his patronage rewarded merit. With the highest exertions of military greatness he united the gentlest offices of humanity.

'His concern for the interest, and unwearied attention to the health, of all his command, softened the necessary exactions of duty and the rigours of discipline by the care of a guardian, and the tenderness of a father.

'Thus belov'd and rever'd, amiable in private life as illustrious in public; this gallant and profitable servant of his country, when he was beginning to reap the harvest of his toils and dangers, in the full meridian of years and glory, having been providentially preserved through ev'ry peril incident to his profession ... died ... and (amidst the groans and tears of his beloved Cornishmen) was here deposited.'

If the Boscawens were the embodiment of honour, integrity and decency, from their home at Tregothnan, then the Hawkins family of Trewithen included the worst counter-elements in that they were associated with some of the most outrageous incidents of vote-rigging in Cornwall's rather unsavoury speciality in this art.

The two Hawkins brothers, John and Christopher, could not have been more different one from another.

John, born in about 1756, was a great academic and traveller who devoted his long life to studying art, literature and science. He was a distinguished member of the Royal Society and wrote a large number of important papers on Cornish geology and related matters. He travelled widely in Greece and Turkey and was, by all accounts, an honoured and revered man who died at Trewithen in July 1841.

Less respected, though, was his younger brother, Christopher,

who was born in 1758 and who, when he was not election-rigging, was a very controversial bachelor who appeared mean to his foes but generous to his friends.

It was said of Trewithen, when he lived there:

> *A large park without deer,*
> *A large cellar without beer,*
> *A large house without cheer,*
> *Sir Christopher Hawkins lives here.*

However, the Cornish historian, Polwhele, takes a rather different view and writes that: 'not a week before his death, I passed a delightful day with the hospitable baronet. To draw around him the few literary characters of his neighbourhood was his peculiar pleasure; and at Trewithen the clergy in particular had always a hearty welcome.'

Way back in the days of the reforms of King Edward VI, tiny Cornish boroughs had been given seats in Parliament so that Crown appointees could play their part. Even worse, the lords of the manor were given the duty of either appointing the actual electors, or of voting for them.

Grampound once had a notorious reputation. Christopher Hawkins of Trewithen represented the borough of Grampound from 1800-1810.

Thus it was not uncommon for Parliamentary representatives to be elected with as many as five votes being split between the two successful candidates!

The buying of votes became a cottage industry, with Sir Christopher Hawkins in the thick of it. Voters were offered a 'breakfast' as an inducement. But 'breakfast' was a polite word for a bribe of £24.

On the eve of the election of 1806, a deputation from one Cornish town went to see Sir Christopher to offer him the goodwill of the electorate or, in other words, to see how much he would pay them to vote for certain candidates.

The delegation was at Trewithen for some hours, a subsequent investigation found, and dined at his table which 'on this occasion was more freely supplied than was the custom on ordinary days'. The result of the election showed a good majority for Sir Christopher's nominees.

The Common Serjeant investigated and Sir Christopher and his colleagues were put up for trial, at Bodmin Assize, in August 1808. Evidence was given that the deputation, representing the voters, had agreed to sell their votes for Sir Christopher's favoured candidates 'for twenty-four guineas apiece paid to themselves, and for ten guineas to be handed to each of the overseers, and that the offer was duly accepted.' On top of that, twenty shillings was to be paid to each individual voter. Since nobody would admit to having been bribed, the prosection case collapsed.

Christopher Hawkins represented Mitchell, in Parliament, from 1784-1799 – when he resigned; Grampound from 1800-1810, and Penryn from 1818-1820, before buying his seat in St Ives in 1821.

Despite his colourful record, he was knighted in 1791, created Recorder of Grampound and St Ives and managed to be the longest-serving Member of Parliament of his day!

He was genuinely interested in Cornish expertise and prowess and, from Richard Trevithick, bought the first portable agricultural steam-thresher ever sold to a British landowner and farmer. Clearly Trewithen was an important proving-bed for Trevithick's invention for a committee of experts reported in 1812: 'Having been requested to witness and report on the effect of steam applied to work a mill for threshing corn at Trewithen, we hereby testify that a fire was lighted under the boiler of the engine five minutes after eight o'clock, and at twenty-five minutes after nine o'clock the threshing mill began to work, in which time one bushel of coal was consumed. That from the time the mill began to work to two minutes after two o'clock, being four hours and three-quarters, fifteen hundred sheaves of barley were threshed clean, and one bushel of coal more was consumed . . . We approve of the steadiness and the velocity with which the machine worked, and in every respect we prefer the power of steam, as here applied, to that of horse.'

Rogue though he may have been, Sir Christopher Hawkins was at least

Trewithen

forward-thinking and, it seems, was missed by those who actually loved and respected him. An obituary prophesied: 'His death will be greatly felt and deplored by hundreds. His charitable contributions amongst the indigent will be found greatly wanting. A more generous and benevolent landlord could not be found. He was never known to distrain on rent.'

He died, at Trewithen, in April 1829.

The Hocking brothers, of St Stephen-in-Brannel, could also claim descent from one of the oldest Cornish families as their mother was a Kitto. Silas, the third son of James Hocking and Elizabeth Kitto took Kitto as his middle name, whereas his brother remained – singularly – John.

James Hocking was part-owner of a tin mine and it was against this social and economic background that Silas, born 1850, and Joseph, born 1860, grew up. Family resources made it possible for both of them to be educated privately and, initially, earmarked for careers as mine surveyors. They were part of a close-knit family and, according to Joseph, dark winter evenings were often spent 'in the old chimney corner, with a log on the fire, and my mother telling me ancient

35

The water tower at Trelissick.

Cornish stories of wizards, wreckers, ghosts and haunted houses.'

Good literature appealed to Joseph and, well before he was twelve years old, he had read all Sir Walter Scott's books. He would walk ten or twelve kilometres to buy a cheap reprint of the classics. When he was thirteen, he wrote his first novel. It was, he said, 'not a success'.

By the time he was twenty, and after studying land surveying, he joined the United Methodist Free Church and served both in the Middle East and as minister of Woodford Green Union church in Essex, resigning in 1910 to develop his talents as a writer.

Although his first book appeared in 1891, he would have seen 53 in print when he died in 1937. He hit upon popular fiction as being an effective way of carrying religious and moral messages to the public and, for a time, saw some of his stories appear in serial form in mass-circulation weekly and monthly magazines.

Many of Joseph's tales were set in the Cornwall he knew and loved so well and, like his mother's yarns in the old chimney corner, drew on the cliff-hanging element of suspense. Joseph Hocking was an undoubted success as a writer. Yet his success was totally over-shadowed by that of his brother, Silas.

At nineteen he gave up his surveying studies and, as Joseph was to do fourteen years later, joined the United Methodist Free Church, serving as minister at Pontypool, Spalding, Liverpool and Manchester before commencing, in 1883, a thirteen-year ministry at Southport. He was a powerful and eloquent preacher and usually attracted capacity congregations wherever he went.

After sixteen years in the ministry, he resigned so that he could concentrate on writing Liberal pamphlets, journalism and lecturing. He twice stood unsuccessfully for Parliament as a Liberal candidate in 1906 and 1910.

While minister at Liverpool, in 1878, he wrote his first book. The second appeared twelve months later and he sold the copyright for the sum of £20, little realising that he had given away the rights to a book for children – *Her Benny* – that was to be translated and sold worldwide in excess of one million copies!

He wrote 50 books and, at one time, became England's best-selling novelist. His attitude, he said, consisted of writing about things he knew best for people who understood those things. In a tribute to his success, Sir Henry Campbell-Bannerman said that he had: ' done more for providing healthy fiction for the young people of this country than any other man.'

If the Hockings were the stars of the nonconformist beliefs of generations of ministers born near, or associated with, the River Fal, then the Church of England can claim equal status through two vicars of Mylor and one of Ruan Lanihorne, Thomas Peters, Thomas Tregosse and John Whitaker.

Thomas Peters was vicar of Mylor for two decades up to his death in 1654. However, due to pressures in the days of Cromwell, he went to America and set up a small church and congregation there before returning to Cornwall. Perhaps his period away made sense in the context of saving his skin rather than merely that of saving souls since one of his relations, Hugh Peters, who had acted as Oliver Cromwell's chaplain was beheaded on Tower Hill on the orders of King Charles II.

Perhaps knowing that his death was imminent, Thomas Peters began his last will and testament in October 1654 in these words: 'I, Thomas Peters, preacher of the Gospell of Jesus Christ for twentie yeares at Mylour in Cornwall, though with little success in soules, being in good and blessed memory (blessed be my Lord Jesus) though having some of deathes sentences upon my body . . .'

Thomas Tregosse, who followed Thomas Peters as vicar of Mylor, was a far more controversial and charismatic pastor – although an acute embarrassment to the church of the day. Having preached at St Ives as a Presbyterian for two years from 1657, he was the rather surprise choice for the joint living of Mylor-with-Mabe, as it was obvious that he could not accept the rigid rules of religious observance of the day when, among other things, it was an offence for a child to sit at the bedside of a mortally-ill grandparent and read comforting prayers or collects. By 1662 things had come to such a head that he was evicted from the living.

Undismayed, he embraced the style and doctrines of the 'free' church and, in addition to leading dissenting congregations in Penryn, Falmouth, Mabe and Mylor probably motivated the founding of Falmouth's continuing strong Baptist tradition. It is not clear, however, if he held the views of the Baptists although the ascendancy of their position in Falmouth coincided with his period of greatest 'alternative' activity.

Since the repression of dissenters had led to an increase in the number of common informers, Thomas Tregosse was regularly informed upon to the authorities. He paid many fines of as much as £200 and served three sentences in Launceston prison and others at Bodmin and Exeter.

But even while imprisoned, he continued to preach and, according to Edmund Calamy: 'He was very cheerful in his own spirit and exceedingly useful to many by his warm discourses and admonitions, cautions and exhortations in all the times of his confinement. He was in custody of the Mareschal of Bodmin as a dangerous and seditious person; but very unjustly, for it could not have been charged upon him that either in his preaching or conference he much enveigh'd against the discipline of Liturgy of the Church. Much less did he meddle with State affairs.

'He preached up to ten sermons a week by which labour he soon wore himself away. He dy'd Jany 18th 1673. He was one of eminent piety and yet (which is remarkable) dated his conversion after he had been some time in the ministry, nay and a sufferer for nonconformity too. He was one whom God signally own'd, not only by being instrumental in the conversion of many souls, but also by remarkable judgements which befel several that were instrumental in his troubles.'

In terms of a long incumbency, then the academic and cleric, John Whitaker, vicar of Ruan Lanihorne from 1777-1808, deserves his own place in the history of the River Fal.

But Whitaker's contribution to Cornwall can be measured in greater ways than the mere passage of time.

Born in Manchester, in 1735, he was ordained at Oxford in 1760, and served in London and Manchester before being appointed to the living of Ruan Lanihorne seventeen years later.

Already a controversial figure, John Whitaker had published several books that had been generally well received, although one critic had drawn attention to 'diffusenesses and untenable hypotheses' and had called the author 'a blockhead', despite his working friendships with Dr Johnson and Edward Gibbon.

A fierce campaigner on moral and national issues, he fought for the social improvement of Manchester and called for the creation of a Manchester Regiment 'to subdue the rebels in the Americas'. At Ruan he wrote his famous three-volume analysis, and defence, of Mary Queen of Scots. He collaborated with Richard Polwhele on *Poems Chiefly by Gentlemen of Devonshire and Cornwall*; wrote prefaces to Bibles; produced massive tomes of history and philosophy; and dabbled in Cornish history as well, each of his publications being hailed for its intellectual approach and conversational presentation.

In his faith, John Whitaker was undoubtedly a very high churchman. His church carried the richest vestments, his diary observed the fasts and the feasts. In his most outstanding work, *The Ancient Cathedral of Cornwall*, he wrote with obvious concern and regret that candles were no longer in use in some Cornish churches and that the dignity of observance had been lowered by abandoning the use of incense.

This brought him into conflict with many of his contemporaries, including most of his own parishioners. He once rebuked the Bishop of Derry for 'loose talk' in his presence.

But perhaps Truro Cathedral is the greatest living monument to John Whitaker since it was he, in his writings on Cornwall, who drew public attention to the fact that Cornwall had not always been part of the diocese of Exeter and had, in fact, once had bishops of its own.

From John Whitaker's research, writing, commitment and urging, the seed grew that flowered into the recreation of a separate diocese and Cornwall's own cathedral.

TREGOTHNAN, TRELISSICK and TREWITHEN
– the great houses and gardens

ARGUABLY they are three of Cornwall's finest houses – each with its own style, characteristics, dignity, history and charm, each with a unique story of its owners and their varied contributions to porcelain, to flowers, to leadership and public life.

Their names? Trelissick, Trewithen and Tregothnan.

Trelissick, described by Jean Stubbs in *Great Houses of Cornwall* as being 'set like a jewel in 376 acres of woods and parklands' is as breathtaking if approached by the road, through an appetiser to its beautiful gardens, as it is when first glimpsed from a passing boat when, in the warmth of a summer's day, it seems to laze at the top of green pastures in a carpet of rich growth unfurling from the shore.

Nikolaus Pesvner notes Trelissick as 'the severest neo-Greek

Trewithen – 'a jewel set in woods and parklands.'

Trelissick – 'it swallowed a fortune.'

mansion in Cornwall', yet its builders and occupiers might well seem to belie the severity of the façade.

It dates back to the mid-1700s when it was built by John Lawrence who had been a captain in the county militia and had served during the Seven Years' War, and who was well known for his 'good nature, convivial habits and wild eccentricities.'

Sadly, history does not develop further knowledge of Captain Lawrence and the extent of his eccentricities is not recorded.

In 1800 Trelissick passed to Ralph Daniell, Member of Parliament for West Looe, and reputedly the richest man in Cornwall in his lifetime. Daniell, known as 'guinea-a-minute Daniell' through his rate of acquiring money, left the house to his son who, after commissioning P F Robinson to incorporate the original structure into a majestic mansion, went to France in 1832 to escape his creditors, having virtually spent his vast fortune on rides, carriage roads and paths through the estate.

The next owner of Trelissick was the then Earl of Falmouth who held it for twelve years or so before selling it to John Davies Gilbert. Mr Gilbert was immensely proud of the gardens of Trelissick and often threw them open so that the public could share his pleasure and pride in them.

Typical of his many acts of generosity was the afternoon in 1848 when he gave a party to some 500 youngsters from all the schools in the neighbourhood and his 'bounty was bestowed on this interesting occasion without any distinction of sect or party.'

They arrived by steamer and, from the landing stage 'were conveyed in waggons, with appropriate banners, whilst other children were seen walking in procession. At length, the whole assembled in front of the mansion, where every preparation was made for their reception. Upwards of one thousand persons, from the neighbourhood and Truro were supposed to be present, and were highly delighted at witnessing the kind manner in which the children were served by Mr Gilbert.

'The weather was most delightful, and an excellent choir of singers was present to enliven the scene. After the juveniles had enjoyed themselves for some time in the lawn and pleasure grounds, the party separated, expressing their gratitude to the gentleman who, since he came to reside in the parish, had exerted himself in every possible way to promote the welfare and happiness of its inhabitants.'

Trelissick remained in the ownership of the Gilbert family for 69 years until, in 1928, it was bought by Mr Leonard Cunliffe, a former governor of the Bank of England.

Trelissick – the severest neo-Greek mansion in Cornwall.'

King Henry VIII's map of Falmouth Haven.

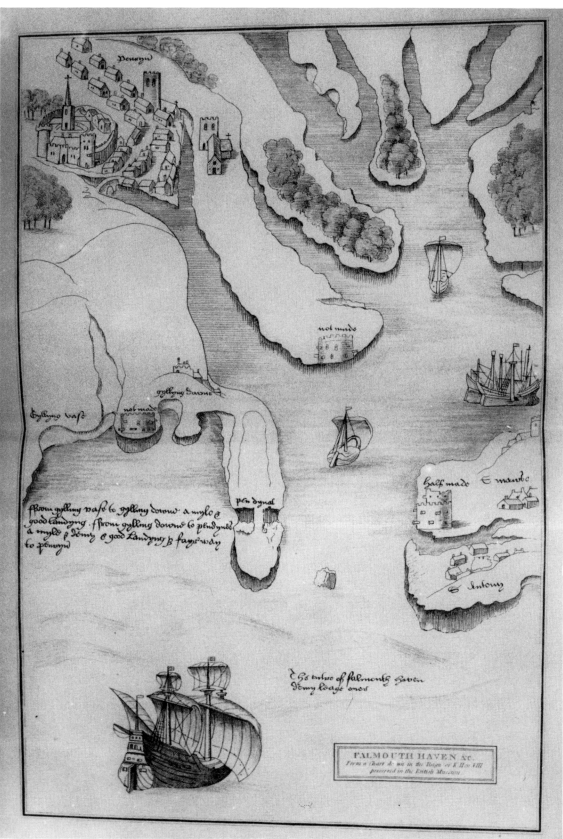

Penryn

not made

gyllyng durne

gyllyng vase

not made

pen dynal

half made   S mande

ffrom gyllyng vase to gyllyng durne a myle &
good landyng. ffrom gyllyng durne to pendynel
a myle & demy & good landyng ys fayr way
to penryn

S Antony

The entre of falmonth haven
demy leage ouer

When he died in 1937, it was left to his step-daughter, Mrs Ida Copeland, who was married to Mr Ronald Copeland, managing director of the famous Spode china factory. It is said that many of the Spode pieces were based on the magnificent blooms which characterise the gardens of Trelissick.

In 1955 Trelissick, together with its park, woods and gardens was given to the National Trust.

One of the features of the grounds – with its cypresses, cedars, and more than 100 varieties of hydrangea – is a fairy-tale like water tower dating back to 1860 when Trelissick was served by its own private reservoir. Nowadays the water tower provides the nearest thing to life in a lighthouse, with one room on each of its four circular floors.

If Trelissick can boast breathtaking gardens, then it has a close rival in Trewithen, near Probus. Trewithen was designed as an impressive residence and was built in the years between 1715 and 1740 as 'a plain and stately house' from local materials, mostly Pentewan stone quarried a few miles away from the cliff-top near Mevagissey.

Its builder, Mr Courtenay Williams, was – like Captain Lawrence, of Trelissick – a bit of a character. It was said that although 'this seat rates among the principal places of Cornwall', Mr Williams himself wasted a great deal of money on 'low pursuits and low company' and

Trelissick in 1831 was called a 'majestic mansion'.

that one of his eccentricities was to have a private team of bellringers who accompanied him from parish to parish to announce his arrival and presence!

But it is in its grounds that Trewithen really comes into its own. According to one expert: 'Without doubt, Trewithen is one of the finest gardens in this county of fine gardens, both for its bold design and for the excellent state of their cultivation.'

It could be said that the design and nurturing of the gardens owed as much to pain and determination as to mere horticultural knowledge on the part of one of its more recent owners, Mr George Johnstone.

Trewithen – 'one of Cornwall's greatest seats.'

Mr Johnstone, an authority on Asiatic magnolias, had introduced every known variety to Trewithen – alongside rare rhododendrons and camellias – when he was severely injured in a hunting accident and spent the rest of his life in a wheelchair. Despite his dreadful disability, he persevered in his determination to make Trewithen a showpiece and, in his wheelchair, went wherever he wished to design his garden and to direct operations.

If the dates of Trewithen and Trelissick can be established, the same is not so of Tregothnan since, although the 'modern' house dates from 1818, it certainly stands on the site of a much earlier house or houses possibly dating back to 1334, or earlier. For it was around that year that the first members of the Boscawen family moved to their grand vantage point above the Fal.

In 1838, there was a recorded reference to the Boscawens and Tregothnan 'whose principal seat it has been ever since 1334 and who have greatly enriched themselves as well as ennobled their blood since that time, by marriages and by matching themselves into the most eminent families of the county.'

In Cornish Tregothnan means 'the place of the well-wooded valleys', and it was at that place that, in 1816, William Wilkins – who was also to design the National Gallery – fashioned a Tudor-styled house incorporating parts of an earlier dwelling dating back some 200 years. By 1842 it was renowned as 'a modern-built house' . . . 'the handsomest seat in Cornwall' . . . and 'the romantic castellated mansion of Tregothnan.'

However, the 'modern-built house' was undeniably much older

Trewithen the home of rare shrubs and trees.

46

than it seemed as it probably replaced the 'noble old mansion' of Pangual mentioned in Domesday Book, and from which the 4th Viscount Boscawen and 1st Earl of Falmouth – Hugh Boscawen – 'carried the stones to build his new house at Tregothnan and a poor farmhouse is built for a tenant in its stead.'

But whether the 'new' house was an act of vandalism on the old; whether the materials were new or recycled; and whether or not some anonymous farmhand was rehoused in sub-standard accommodation is academic. What emerged, in the words of Davies Gilbert, was 'the finest gentleman's seat in Cornwall, with the exception perhaps of Mount Edgcumbe. The house standing there till within these few years bore the appearance of considerable antiquity and harmonised with the surrounding scenery. The replacement may compete with the best in England for real utility and for decorations harmonising with its bold situation and surrounding landscape.'

But, over the years, others had admired earlier Tregothnans. The diarist, Celia Fiennes, called there to see her cousin during her great journey in the autumn of 1698.

She found a 'pleasant house' well ahead of its time in terms of creature comforts. It had two parlours, a smoking-room and a drawing-room that opened onto the garden. Bedrooms were 'newly decorated in the latest manner with damask covers on the beds, one

The mellow face of Trewithen.

47

A charming old photograph of Tregothnan in 1910.

red, one green and one embroidered.' A balcony looked out over the park and, from the top floor, she enjoyed a wide vista leading to Falmouth Bay and around to a landscape with 'hills full of Copper mines'.

The park – with its celebrated chestnut trees – was of some 116 acres and was famous for its herd of some 200 fallow deer.

One of the earlier visitors to 'modern' Tregothnan was Barclay Fox, the great Quaker, from Falmouth. In 1832 and 1833 it proved a popular place for a picnic although, as he wrote on June 26, 1833, life could be hazardous even on a picnic on a calm day:

'About half past twelve we set off for Tregothnan with a most splendid wind which took us up in an hour, everybody enjoying it but Dame Banks who was sick, frightened & fidgety & moreover had a tumble by sitting on a loose winch. After taking some bread and cheese we wandered over Tregothnan house & grounds for about an hour.' Tregothnan, he wrote later, was the ideal place for ' a charming excursion and to dine on the grass.'

But Tregothnan was a place of history and spectacle as well as the scene of leisurely picnics.

In May 1880 it accommodated the Prince and Princess of Wales when they visited Truro for the benediction of the nave of Truro Cathedral. Leaving the Royal train, the Prince and Princess found a relaxed and welcoming atmosphere.

According to *The Royal Cornwall Gazette*: 'The police exercised no irritating restraint on the people and the reception of the Prince and Princess, though maybe lacking in splendour, dignity and grace, yet was full of sincerity and honest enthusiasm. An impromptu flying escort of one hundred cycles fell in behind the Royal carriage and accompanied it to Tregothnan Lodge, where one adventurous cyclist dismounted under the heads of the horses in the second carriage, and the near horse put its foot through the spokes of the hind wheel.'

On the night following the benediction there was – again as *The Royal Cornwall Gazette* reported: 'a ball on a magnificent scale, given by Lord and Lady Falmouth in honour of their Royal visitors. The company numbered three hundred and the affair, which was of a most brilliant character, passed off very successfully, save that some slight inconvenience was experienced from the crowded state of the rooms.'

Next afternoon there was a spectacular garden party, with a military band playing on the lawns.

On the Sunday, having been present for a milestone in the creation of Cornwall's great cathedral, the Prince and Princess joined ordinary villagers and estate workers at the church of St Michael Penkevil.

Once more, *The Royal Cornwall Gazette* captured the occasion in positively romantic prose: 'St Michael's church, nestling amid the trees and beneath the shadows of the beautiful seat of Lord Falmouth, lay sunning itself peacefully amid its rural beauty. Sunshine and shadow kept alternately throwing up and deepening the beauties of the woods and fields, the hills and the valleys, but not a zephyr whispered through the wealth of mid-summer foliage to disturb the peacefulness of the scene. The crow of the pheasant, the twitter of the birds, the occasional bark of a watch-dog in the distance were the only sounds that seemed to throw up into greater relief the peacefulness of the scene ... the village bells sent out their summons to worship. And now, from all parts of the countryside, well-dressed and bright-faced country-folk come tripping in. Their demeanour was orderly and respectful and devotional. It was little more to witness than a customary Sabbath-day picture of country life except, here and there, walked an officer of the law with his blue uniform. His presence seemed an anachronism amid so quiet and well-behaved an assembly.'

And, in a later visit to Tregothnan, the next Prince and Princess of Wales were rowed up the Fal, in 1903, by Lord Falmouth's boatmen in their traditional uniforms of white trousers and jackets, red cloaks and dark straw hats.

It was, indeed, 'a house imposingly embosomed in majestic wood, to be considered as one of the most romantic spots in the kingdom ... built on a gentle eminence, commanding a great variety of extensive and dignified prospects, which are greatly improved by the winding courses of the river Fal.'

THE COMMUNITIES AND BYGONE DAYS OF THE FAL

DEVORAN shows few signs of its former greatness as a bustling port associated with Cornwall's mighty tin industry. Through its now virtually untraceable wharves and quays precious tin ore was shipped outwards, with ships taking the ore having first discharged their cargoes of coal, limestone and pit props.

Behind the bustling wharves stood serried ranks of warehouses and sheds; a network of small docks seemed to be guarded by the tall sentinels of cranes and gantries; and chubby bollards punctuated the quaysides. It was even the terminus of a mineral railway which ran up the Carnon valley into the heart of the mines working tin and copper

The port of Devoran as it neared the end of its useful life.

Devoran's wharves.

in the great days before the collapse of mining in the 19th century.

In the tidal stream, locally-owned steamers and tugs pulled barges and ketches using one of Cornwall's main river ports as Devoran replaced Penryn in importance in the late 1820s after an unusually long period of thought and commitment.

It was in 1794 that its potential was first recognised as the ideal place to cope with the mining trade, a grandiose scheme being put in motion to create a tracery of canals to link the mines of the parish of Gwennap with the river. By 1810 that line of thinking had been abandoned in the light of engineering surveys. In 1820, however, the railway link became a reality and within six years it was fully operational. For twenty years, between 1845 and 1865, the facilities grew both in size and in the volume and value of cargoes handled . . . only to wither and gradually peter out as the mining boom peaked and then declined.

Barclay Fox, visiting the port in 1839, wrote excitedly of the introduction of two useful inventions of the local engineer, Captain Tregaskes: 'one for discharging vessels with dispatch, the other for deepening shallow rivers. Both are in operation at Devoran & by the

Barclay Fox.

Reminders of a river port and Devoran's industrial past still protrudes above the water line.

aid of the latter they have already deepened the river in front of our right.'

Three years later, he noted in his diary that he had spent an hour at Devoran 'with Henry Francis, agent to the Railway Co., in convincing him that they had no right to build a dam across the river on our freehold. He accordingly suspended the operation till I should see & talk with R. Taylor, one of the directors.'

The growing popularity of Devoran as a commercial and residential centre was spotlighted by a typical property advertisement of the period referring to the premises for sale as being 'immediately above the new port and quays at Devoran, on the Redruth rail road, and very convenient for a person engaged in mining or mercantile pursuits; or it may be converted, at a trifling expense, into a complete *cottage orné* for a genteel family, commanding beautiful and picturesque views over Carclew Park and Perran and Restronguet Creeks.'

In 1859 Devoran was recognised by the Board of Trade by the provision of an officially approved public barometer for the use of seafarers.

But, by 1870, the end was in sight.

One of the vessels that served the port of Devoran.

The mines were closing, cargoes in decline, shipping traffic falling off. Where once there were 30 ships in port or awaiting a berth, days passed without any. Where once eighteen steam engines at just one mine hungered for coal imported through Devoran, only two remained active. Where five loaded trains had once run in each direction every day between mines and wharves, the number had dwindled to two.

Even worse was the fact that, allowing for food, stores, equipment and a few drinks in the Robartes Arms or other hostelries, each ship handled represented about £10 spending power for the local traders. The financial loss was more than the port could carry and the decline accelerated. In 1877, *The West Briton* noted: 'The trade at this little port of Devoran is in a miserable plight just now. It has wonderfully fallen off, and, in fact, where ten vessels used to enter and discharge, scarcely one does now . . . It may be almost said that the whole district is shut up from a mining point of view, and the consequence is that there is no copper ore to ship at Devoran as formerly, and no coal brought back.'

Just one train a day was now needed to carry the imports and exports of the whole district.

Devoran in 1989 and 'few signs of its former greatness.'

Devoran's decline as a port meant 'less cash for the tills of pubs.' Nowadays The Old Quay Inn, overlooking the river and recently refurbished, caters for a very different type of clientele to that of earlier this century.

The newspaper, perhaps rather stating the obvious, concluded: 'Better times are anxiously longed for.'

Sadly the better times did not come for the mines and, by 1887, the picture was very similar to that described by William Beckford exactly 100 years earlier: 'the consolidated mines ... are situated in a bleak desert, rendered still more doleful by the unhealthy appearance of its inhabitants. At every step one stumbles upon ladders that lead to utter darkness, or funnels that exhale warm copperous vapours.'

Mylor, too, was in the doldrums following the loss of the Royal Naval training ship *Ganges* and the effective closure of its proudest claim to fame, Britain's smallest Royal Naval dockyard.

Mylor Creek had been earmarked as a safe anchorage from as far back as 1533 and had, over the years, been the scene of boatbuilding and other maritime activities connected with fishing and the carriage of a wide range of cargoes.

In the early 1800s the former private enterprise Falmouth Packet service of mailships had moved into Admiralty control. It was decided that, in the interests of convenience, economy and efficiency, a Royal Naval dockyard should be established at Mylor for repairs to existing

Packet ships and for the conversion of rather old and structurally suspect brigs-of-war to a new role.

With the frigate *Astraea* anchored off Mylor, in Carrick Roads, as a floating store-ship and headquarters, work started on building a dockyard on marshland literally beneath the walls of Mylor church. Facilities would include capacity for making barrels for food, water and drink; ropes and sails; the storage of ammunition; and for carpenters and shipwrights.

By 1805, with the battle of Trafalgar still some months away and victory over the French beyond the horizon of foreseeable expect-ation, the modest plan had become expanded and accelerated to encompass a slipway, officers' accommodation, a guard-house for Royal Marines, a smithy, an iron-foundry and even an embryonic military hospital.

By 1823, Mylor was the scene of early government surplus sales, with 'several tons of double-headed shot' being available 'by sealed tender to the King's Cooperage, Mylor.'

Twelve years later, in 1835, the Lords of the Admiralty allocated repairs to all ships carrying packets to the yard rather than splitting the task with Plymouth.

By 1843, with Mylor Royal Naval dockyard a reality, it was decided

HMS Ganges, the old naval training ship which was anchored off Mylor.

Mylor Creek in 1909 and a pleasure boat noses her way upstream with a cargo of eager sightseers.

that *HMS Astraea* could be released for duties at Southampton. There was a grand farewell celebration and dinner . . . but next day the signal was countermanded and she was allowed to stay, with her Master acting as superintendent of the dockyard as well.

One of his first duties in this dual role was the bizarre task, in 1845, of creating a graveyard to the north of Mylor churchyard to be made available for the bodies of those who either drowned in the harbour; were washed up on the shore; or who died upon ship. Although the reason for this was that, officially, pressure on burial space was already too great in the area, it seems that there was growing local awareness of the possibility that seamen might be suffering from, or carriers of, infectious disease.

The dockyard was run-down and closed for a short period in the early 1850s, but was recommissioned and refurbished in 1854 as a result of increased naval activity and the need to have a casualty facility west of Plymouth capable of dealing with emergency repairs and storm damage.

The Royal Naval training ship *Ganges* arrived off Mylor in 1866. Those who saw her arrive in the tow of the tug *Gladiator* were not to know that she would be the centre of attention and embarrassment as the result of the harsh discipline enforced by her Master, Commander Stevens.

Ganges was not a new ship. She had been built and launched at Bombay 45 years earlier. Conditions were primitive, facilities few. Boys rose at half past five. After breakfast – hot cocoa without milk or sugar, and biscuits infested with weevils, or dried bread with dripping – they carried out physically exhausting drill involving manning the masts and yard-arms, and setting and stowing sail. The second morning session covered seamanship and gunnery until twenty minutes to twelve when there was Captain's muster, followed by lunch of meat and potatoes with cabbage and doughboys. More hard training went on throughout the afternoon, followed by the last meal of the day – tea and bread-and-treacle – at four o'clock.

With tea out of the way, there were a further two hours of intensive physical recreation, followed by either a cross-country run or a spell rowing a long-boat.

Tough though this programme was, it was the seemingly innocuous Captain's muster that held the greatest menace. During this assembly, a Court of Inquiry found there was some truth in reports that Commander Stevens had 'given punishments beyond those laid down in Training Regulations.'

This rather bland statement covered investigations into the fact that Captain's muster had become an almost daily ritual in which, through tiredness, exhaustion or even accident, lads who had seemingly fallen short of the Commander's high standards were publicly rebuked for offences against discipline and sentenced to a variety of punishments ranging from seven days in solitary confinement for singing a bawdy song to laying a lad across a gun and

A memorial to HMS Ganges trainees who did not stay the course aboard the ships where conditions were primitive and facilities few. Many of the lads lived but some died.

birching him with a cane dipped in brine for petty theft.

One distressed local mother, a Mrs Finch, went to Mylor with a big club with the intention of sorting Commander Stevens out! When he sent a message saying that he was unable to see her, she waited for the arrival of a new intake of trainees – and successfully persuaded them to go home. They were lucky. As a memorial in Mylor churchyard recalls, many died.

Commander Stevens was relieved his command of *Ganges* and transferred to other duties.

In the meantime, *Ganges* had become the host ship for many important occasions and visitors and entered into community life with teams of young sailors joining in local football contests, taking

Overleaf: A complement of HMS Ganges. Ropes are coiled with precision but some of the trainees in the background look decidedly grubby and out-at-elbows.

59

part in regattas, and doing many voluntary acts for the benefit of the immediate neighbourhood.

In 1888 she went to Devonport, under tow, for an extensive survey and for work on re-coppering her bottom. Although she was pronounced fit on her return to Mylor, rumours began to circulate that she was to be withdrawn from service. An Admiralty spokesman admitted that although there was a pretty strong hint that this might be the case, 'Official secrecy bars any access to any dependable confirmation or denial.'

Replying to local protests about the growing belief that she was to be moved, the Admiralty said that the position was under review for sanitary reasons; general training policy on the training of boy seamen; and the shortage of Westcountry lads enlisting.

Although each of these claims was resisted and contradicted in the light of powerful evidence, the Admiralty came clean, in August 1899, that she was to leave.

On August 31, 1899, taken in tow by a tug, *Ganges* slipped her moorings and made for St Anthony and the open sea. *The West Briton* was on hand to record the occasion: 'Just before her arrival off St Mawes castle she dipped her ensign twice as a farewell signal to the port, a signal which was answered by the soldiers at Pendennis castle.'

In 1930 the Admiralty finally relinquished its presence at Mylor, although the tiny dockyard saw service again in the 1939-45 war as a base for units of the Free French navy and, in 1944, for preparations for the invasion of Europe, by the United States Navy.

While Restronguet is, perhaps, best-known for its picturesque and popular Pandora Inn, the name – although historic – is of comparatively recent origin compared with the history of the house itself.

Dating back more than 200 years, it was originally known as the Passage House Inn, serving those who crossed the river by ferry at that point. In 1789, it seems, a fisherman named Thomas Harvey took on the lease of 'a cottage or dwelling house called the Passage House adjoining the Beach at Restrongett Passage, together with the stable and pigs at one end of the said dwelling house . . . also all that ferry or passage called Restrongett Passage together with the two Boats, Ores, Ropes, Grapples and Materials thereto belonging, and the liberty of passing and repassing . . . to the opposite shore or beach in the passage of Feock and back again according to the ancient usage and customary right now and heretofore uninterruptedly exercised and enjoyed by former lessees of the said ferry or passage.'

Although the ferry continues to this day, the name of the inn was changed to The Ship in the eighteenth century and, swiftly and more specifically, to The Pandora.

HMS Ganges – 'an attraction and embarassment'.

After the mutiny on *HMS Bounty* had resulted in Captain Bligh being cast adrift in a small boat some seven metres long, and successfully navigating and covering an incredible 7,030 kilometres in six weeks, the Admiralty was determined to track down the mutineers who had taken the ship.

Captain Edward Edwards was ordered to take the 24-gun frigate, *HMS Pandora*, to arrest the men and bring them back to Britain for a court martial. Lacking the knowledge and experience of Captain Bligh, he only sailed to Tahiti where he found half the mutineers, little realising that the other group had made their way to Pitcairn Island.

Although Bligh had been a disciplinarian, he had a reputation for fairness and good seamanship. Edwards seemingly lacked both and, throughout the voyage, insisted that his prisoners be kept in leg-irons and manacles in a tiny cubicle on the ship's deck – known popularly, but without affection as 'Pandora's Box'. However, on the voyage home, *HMS Pandora* sank.

It was thus Edwards, himself, who faced a court martial. He was found guilty of negligence and dismissed the service, moving into the old Ship Inn at Restronguet and changing its name to The Pandora Inn.

In Edwards' days, and for many years afterwards, Restronguet Pool was a busy scene of shipping activity. Timber brought from Norway to the mines of Gwennap was unloaded there and taken by raft up the creek to the most convenient point of discharge. The Norway Inn takes its name from these activities.

Despite their very fine reputation for seaworthiness and upkeep, not all Norwegian ships were in the peak of condition.

In July 1859, the brig *Marthe Andrea*, was declared to be a total loss through negligence. On her voyage from Norway she sprang a leak, and was put in drydock near Restronguet for the re-caulking of her seams and for a general survey. Unfortunately she was not secured and twisted in the dry dock, thus straining and damaging the hull in such a way that she had to be condemned as unseaworthy.

Not only was Lars Berg her captain, he owned the brig as well. Unable to face up to the loss of his livelihood as well as his ship and his reputation, he walked to the riverside, tied a heavy stone around his chest, and jumped in. The inquest jury decided he had killed himself while temporarily insane.

'The picturesque and popular Pandora Inn captured on camera in 1905. Nowadays it wears a somewhat different face but the attraction remains the same.

The old Ship Inn became the Pandora Inn.

There is no trace, nowadays, of the eight-towered castle that once dominated Ruan Lanihorne, and little outward evidence of the historic status of the village as a major river port on the Fal.

The castle was demolished many centuries ago, but its masonry was used in building the church and in many local houses.

When Tregony became silted-up, Ruan Lanihorne took over responsibility for being the last up-river point for shipping, some six dried-out kilometres downstream. It became, through Tregony's misfortune, a busy and important place able to accommodate ships of 80 to 100 tons – and even, on occasions, three-masters. But the march of the silt down the Fal continued and the era of greatness began to fail about 1730.

At the beginning of the eighteenth century, H L Douch recalls in *Old Cornish Inns*, one of the oldest inhabitants of Ruan Lanihorne gave his recollection of the Cornish sport of hurling. In this, a contest between two parishes or two villages, a ball is hurled from person to person in a cross-country scramble in which the victor is the man who survives the guile, the speed (and the toughness) of his opponents to reach the goal at the end of the course.

Billy Simmons told how: 'of this, the long-settled Ruanites talk much; and seem to glory in the prowess of their ancestors at this work.

Overleaf: Ruan Lanihorne in 1890. It was a busy and important place when Tregony died.

65

The silver ball as it was called was in reality a common ball of yarn with threads of silver intertwined upon the surface, and was kept in the parish for this diversion and was laid up every year in the church chest. This was thrown up at the centre of the ring. It was caught in its descent by one of the upper or the lower party. The Lowlanders were to hurl it down the hill and the Highlanders to hurl it up. Great dexterity in catching and great activity in hurling must be necessary in such a contest. Certain laws were prescribed to prevent any unfairness of operation, and to preclude any violence of brutality. Under such restraints the exercise would be good and the exertion animated. The contest was generally friendly in fact ... the damage between the two goals, to which the contending parties were striving to hurl the ball, were a broken pane for the Lowland men and within the lone house of Treworga at the Three Gates for the Highland.'

St Just-in-Roseland, although far more famous for its beautiful church and churchyard, also has an interesting link with the history of the Fal as it was, on several occasions, seen as the possible concluding-point of a minerals railway running from the heart of the china clay world of the upper-Fal to a china clay loading facility in St Just Pool.

In the 1870s, the Cornwall Minerals Railway Company decided to

St Just in Roseland Church in 1906.

St. Anthony's Lighthouse.

Carrick Road in 1910. There were plans laid for a major port.

revise and reconsider an existing scheme that would have seen a railway running from Bodinnick and St Stephen's Coombe. Under the updated thinking, a line would run from Retew to Newquay in one direction, and to St Just Pool in the other, following the line of the Fal as far as possible.

However, a slump in the china clay industry led to the schemes being postponed indefinitely.

By 1910, though, delays in loading at Fowey were causing the china clay companies to re-examine the possibilities of St Just. A Parliamentary Select Committee approved the St Just Ocean Wharves and Railways Bill despite fierce opposition from the port interests of Fowey, the Falmouth Docks Company and the Great Western Railway. By the time approval had been obtained, the problems at Fowey had been resolved and the St Just Pool project, involving a beautiful area of water 'designed and made by the Almighty for the use of man', was abandoned.

St Stephen-in-Brannel suffers, more than any other Cornish town, from a crisis of identity. It has been recorded as St Stephen in Branel, St Stephen in Branwell and St Stephen in Bernel.

Certainly the last name has a strong claim to authenticity as that is the one by which the important manor house, recorded in Domesday, was known before it became more popularly known as Branel. However, the meaning of 'Branel' is not obvious. What is apparent, though, is the ruggedness and individuality of its townspeople through the ages.

In 1793 its miners marched to Lostwithiel and persuaded the authorities to release a colleague who had been sent to prison for mobilising opposition to a massive rise in the price of corn due to shortages having been created by the export of local crops rather than using them in the locality.

In November 1810, Alexander Truscott avoided going to prison for cutting down trees owned by the lord of the manor by publishing a timely and grovelling apology as a warning to others 'not to be guilty of a similar offence. Now I do hereby most sincerely acknowledge my sorrow for having committed the said offence, and my thankfulness for the lenity that has been shown to me.'

Edward Coad, who went from St Stephen to Illinois in search of work wrote home, in 1819, of having found: 'the most beautiful country that I ever saw; the prairies level and grass plenty, surrounded by woods, very handy for building houses and fences. The houses are all of timber, and so are almost all the fences. I would not pursuade any persons to come here; let them observe their own mind.'

There were well-paid jobs, he said, for masons, blacksmiths, shoemakers, carpenters and tailors.

And, he advised: 'If any of our friends are coming to America, let them provide for themselves boxes to put their provisions and clothes in, and find for themselves on their passage; for it is the cheapest and best way.'

No doubt there was quite an outflow of residents when they learned, in 1829, of a St Stephen's woman who was attacked by a rat and which tore at her cheek and held on until help arrived. She was found, covered in blood, and with her face marked for life.

It seems that publicans had to work hard to keep ahead of the successful activities of the teetotallers and that, in 1832, worshippers leaving St Stephen-in-Brannel church were greeted by the town crier, standing in the churchyard, and advertising the fact that good beer was now on sale at a neighbouring hostelry at very competitive prices!

Three years later an elderly man, George Trethewey, startled market-goers when he turned up with his young wife – secured by a halter around her waist – and solemnly put her up for auction. After two bids, she was sold for four pence to a tinker who took her off to a pub for a celebratory drink.

Mr Trethewey paid the one penny fee charged at the market for the sale of pigs and other animals, and then set his sights on a replacement wife.

Tinkers and gipsies could often earn a fortune from the superstitious and rather gullible people of the china clay area. In 1846,

St Stephen-in-Brannel and the face of the village post office in 1910.

71

having convinced a St Stephen's farmer that someone had put a spell on him, two female gipsies then offered to remove it for the sum of £2. He paid up, but the spell in the form of rheumatism, persisted so he agreed to increase the fee to £7 as they said they had never before had such hard work and that release would cost all the gold he could possibly scrape together.

Reacting to his obvious concern that they might disappear with the coins with the de-spelling incomplete, the gipsies said that there was no problem as they would wrap them in linen cloth, fasten the cloth and the coins to his back, and leave them there until midnight a week later when the pain would have gone and the sovereigns would have doubled.

For the length of the treatment, he was not aware that the rheumatism was easing. Still, he thought, the money was safe – he could feel it – and it would soon be doubled.

At midnight on the appointed night he had to admit that the pain was as bad as ever – although at least the money would be compensation. He undid the linen package ... and found that the gipsies had switched farthings for sovereigns.

St Stephen-in-Brannel and 'a call at the Queen's' in 1900.

THE POT-WALLOPERS AND VOTE-RIGGERS OF TREGONY

OF this there can be no doubt. Of all the communities flanking the banks of the River Fal, Tregony is the oldest. It was there long before Truro and well before Penryn. It existed in the days of Ptolemy who refers to it as Cenionis Ostium.

It requires a feat of superhuman and intuitive imagination to even begin to visualise it as the important, busy, prosperous and influential place it was in its early years when the river lapped its quays and wharves; when businesses flourished; and when its waters ran swift and deep without the intrusion of a mining industry that brought wealth to other communities yet congealed Tregony's water arteries in a thrombosis of creeping and deepening silt.

Almost in the spirit of King Canute – as if man could halt, hold or reverse nature – two Acts of Parliament were passed in the days of King Henry VII in the hope that the thickening waters could be

A Tregony pub in 1904. Once there were 36 pubs in the town.

diluted, the wastes dispersed, and maritime trade could continue. But it was to no avail.

It is said that the debris of minerals destroyed the ancient church, by undermining its foundations and causing its collapse. It had, too, its castle, built by the Norman family of Pomeray in the days of St Stephen, the last of the Norman kings.

By 1295 Tregony had joined Launceston, Bodmin, Truro, and Liskeard in the right to send two of its burgesses to seats in Parliament. It was, however, possibly with a feeling of practical relief rather than injured pride that Tregony lost its seats to Lostwithiel many years later. The five hundred kilometres from Tregony to Westminster were hard, tiring and dangerous to man, to horse and to coach. The journey took as long as four days in each direction and the pay was 10d (4½p) per day while actually at Westminster or on the journey to or from London. Small wonder that few Members ever sought re-election for a second term of office!

Domestic matters worried the burgesses of Tregony when, in 1630, a report was made to Cornwall Assizes that, despite a small population, public facilities included 36 alehouses. The burgesses were directed to 'take into them the consideration of how many shall be licensed there'.

Young girls pose beside the bridge at Tregony in 1909.

From the look of this chap early this century he was off to seek his fortune with stick and bundle.

In the 1830s, Tregony was rather grandly described as 'formerly a place of some consequence. It had two churches, a castle and a priory; but one of the churches, St James's, at the bottom of the town, has long since gone to decay, and the one remaining at the head of the town, has a respectable and venerable appearance. Scarcely a vestige remains of the castle, which stood at the lower end of the town. This fortress is said to have been built by Henry de Pomeroy, on behalf of John Earl of Cornwall, at the time that King Richard I was in the Holy Land, it was standing and was the seat of the Pomeroys, in the reign of Edward VI.

'In the year 1696, Hugh Boscawen, Esq., founded an hospital for decayed housekeepers, and endowed it with lands, now let at 30£. per annum, but capable of being raised (at the expiration of the present lease) to about three times that sum.

'Tregony returned members to Parliament in the reign of Edward I, and the right of election is vested in the principal house-keepers who pay scot and lot. According to the last census, the inhabitants amount to 1035, being an increase of only 112 since the year 1811. Tregony has a market weekly, and five fairs annually.

'On the north-west side of the town stood what is called Old Tregony, where was a church dedicated to St James, the walls of which were standing when Tonkin made his collections about the year 1736; part of the tower remained many years later. The church was a rectory, the advowson of which belonged to the Abbey de Valle in Normandy, and was given by that convent in the year 1267, to the prior and convent of Merton in Surrey, together with the Prior of Tregony, a small cell to that alien monstery. Mr Whitaker says that the site of the

Tregony's 'very fine public clock'.

75

Tregony School – little changed outside since it was built.

Priory of Tregony was opposite the old mount of the castle: and speaks of a doorway belonging to a stable as having been the gateway of the Priory.'

In 1761, some tin-miners working through part of the burial-ground of the former St James's church uncovered a coffin. The fact that it contained a giant skull came as little surprise for the coffin was almost four metres long and over one metre deep and contained what had obviously been the body of a real-life giant. It was not possible to preserve the skeleton for, as the air entered the opened lid, the bones disintegrated into dust – other than in the case of one huge tooth that somehow survived.

While Tregony enjoyed its status as a town returning representatives to Westminster, its reputation was inversely related to its influence. Election-time was an occasion for lying, cheating, perjury, bribery, and all the other niceties of a rotten borough. It was said that 'visions of election money disinclined Tregony men from honest industry which only promised bread in return for honest work.'

Much depended upon the length of the election campaign. If the dissolution took place unexpectedly, the drunkenness and idleness lasted a shorter time indeed, but were only the more intense because the fun was only enjoyable from the issuing of the writ to the end of the fifteen days poll; if the Parliament died a natural death, or if the Sovereign's health gave cause for alarm long before a fatal termination, then the inconvenience to the neighbourhood was prolonged, agents or even candidates appeared in the borough, or their coming was confidently foretold. In any case men's minds were in a state of excitement, and public houses opened their taps with unwonted liberality to the destruction of all decency and the neglect of all common means of earning a livelihood.'

Yet, despite the deceit and the double-selling or auctioning of voting pledges, Tregony was beginning to come to its senses just as the fruits of dishonour were slipping away.

Some 30 years before the town was disenfranchised, *The West Briton* noted, on October 9, 1812: 'Tregony has most unexpectedly shewed symptoms of deserting the old interest and voting against the proprietor of the borough. The right of election here is in all the householders, commonly called "pot-boilers", or "pot-wallopers", and after having kept their plans secret for some time, lest they should be turned out before the dissolution of Parliament; they suddenly turned round, and invited *somebody* to stand for the borough. They have found two persons, and if they can "raise the wind", they will be returned, if not, the landed property will prevail.'

Materialistic though many townspeople may have been when it came to selling their votes, Tregony had a reputation for community generosity when tragedy struck or need arose.

In May 1820, Nicholas Boase lost his home, barn, stables, equipment, wheat, barley and outhouses in a blaze. The value was put at being as much as £400. Even worse, his insurance had just run out! At a public meeting in the Queen's Head, it was resolved: 'that respectable persons be requested to solicit contributions within their respective neighbourhoods, and that printed particulars and forms be sent to each for that purpose.'

Mr Boase was restored to business probably because he was able to rely upon others at his time of need – and was not disappointed. Another man was not surprised, it is hoped, at the opposite response to an action based on greed.

At the Cornwall Summer Assizes of August 1831 he faced trial charged with selling a clapped-out old horse to a man who desperately needed one.

It transpired that a Mr Reynolds saw a horse being ridden by a Mr Vincent and decided it would be ideal for his requirements. He had a trial ride and, after negotiating, went to Mr Vincent's house for a few drinks and to seal the price at £10.

In a rather bemused state he rode home. Next day he found that, as opposed to the fine horse he thought he had bought, he was now the possessor of 'a pig-mouthed old mare with a bad spavin', and totally unsuited to his needs.

Tregony almshouses.

He went back to Mr Vincent for a refund; was refused; and took him to Court where he was awarded £3 damages.

Although St James's church had long disappeared, Tregony still observed the feast of St James as a major date in its community calendar, one of the highlights of the celebration being the annual election of a 'sham' mayor. This was an occasion for a rowdy, hilarious and generally-good-natured day of public drinking centred about the mayor-making.

In October 1835, the 'rites and dignities' of the mayoralty fell on the sexton of the parish. Newspapers tell that: 'His worship, who is very fond of "heavy wet", indulged himself on this occasion with a greater quantum than usual; in consequence of which, we regret to state, he slipt his foot in descending from a vehicle in which he had been drawn about the town, and the wheel passing over him, broke his leg.'

If Tregony was proud of anything, it was of its very fine public clock. And it was with a real sense of outrage that it was discovered, early on a December morning in 1861, that hooligans had smashed in the door and stolen the weights and pendulum.

To avoid any repeat or copy-cat act, the clock-keeper, Mr Bawden, to 'the cheers of an assemblage of a great number of men, women and children', took possession of the clock, the bell, the dials and the vane and carried them to a secure place of custody.

'The people', it was reported, 'are still in a very excited state, and the present appearance of the clock turret is very deplorable.'

There is no record as to whether or not the culprits were found. However, had they been, they might well have spent six hours in the public stocks which were in use in Tregony until the mid-1860s.

Another point of concern was the width of the old road bridge at the foot of the town over the Fal. Over the years farm carts had been becoming wider, whereas the clearance between the inward-jutting buttresses of the bridge was only two-and-a-half metres. This provided a straight choice of either getting strong men to lift a laden cart, wheel-by-wheel over the obstructions, or else of making a six-kilometre detour through Grampound or Probus to circumnavigate less than 20 metres of the important road to Truro.

Farmers had already widened their gates and replaced stiles to accommodate newer agricultural implements, but Tregony bridge remained stubborn, inconvenient, narrow and impassable.

But if Tregony had problems of access, it certainly had advantages in education.

An 1864 survey announced that while, in the mining districts of Cornwall, provision and resources were poor, rural areas – such as Tregony – were well catered for. In Truro, it was found, there were ten schools to cater for 1,104 children. Tregony, with a parish population of 6,100 had nine schools for 563 children, rather less than one school for 60 youngsters. The mining parishes, however, could only muster eight schools for 650 children.

Although trailing in many things, Tregony was at least providing for a good future for its young people.

The 'new' bridge at Tregony.

ST CUBY, ST KEA, ST MELORUS — AND SUSANNAH DANIELL

EVEN if stories of a crock of gold, of several lesser-known saints; and a living flower-show of colourful and exotic growth can be ignored, the churches that look out over the Fal are as quaint, fascinating and individually beautiful as any in Cornwall.

Take St Michael Penkevil, for instance, consecrated in 1261 by Bishop Bronescombe, of Exeter, and of which the original foundation stone can still be seen.

It is a dignified memorial to generations of the Boscawens, of Tregothnan, but allows outside history to intrude as well in the form of a lectern carved by Belgian craftsmen who were refugees in Cornwall after their homeland had been invaded by the Germans in 1914. Then there is a brass figure of a kneeling knight, the work of Mary Gillick, whose other claim to fame is that she was responsible for the portrait of Queen Elizabeth II that appeared on the face of coins struck in the first years of her reign.

St Michael Penkevil church – 'every feature jealously preserved.'

Following Bishop Bronescombe's consecration, St Michael Penkevil seems to have weathered rather more rapidly than its builders anticipated for, in the records for 1319, is a deed recording that Sir John Trejagu had 'at his own cost now recently altogether repaired the said church' of which he was patron.

In addition to making good the structural defects, Sir John funded a chantry for four chaplains so that perpetual prayers could be offered

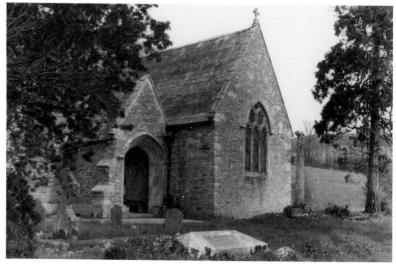

Lamorran Church looks like a film set.

The historic font at Ruan Lanihorne Church.

for himself; his wife; his parents; and the then Bishop and clergy of the diocese of Exeter.

By 1355, though, the fabric was playing up again and the call went out for top-up grants, Pope Benedict XII giving the go-ahead to raise money from the faithful to those 'who have held forth an assisting hand to the fabric, lights, ornaments or any other necessaries.'

The modern church dates from 1862, when George Edmund Street was given the rather tightly-drawn requirement that he should faithfully restore St Michael Penkevil 'with the condition that every old feature be jealously preserved and carefully brought to light and that additions to the old work should be made where it had already been so far defaced as to make the attempt to restore the existing work a mistaken and useless labour.'

The condition about jealously preserving every old feature was, no doubt, based on a fascinating historical footnote in which – some 400 years ago – St Michael Penkevil became the first recorded church to be vandalised in Cornwall, albeit in the cause of recycling!

In the days of Henry VIII, a local man named Carminow wanted a slab to cover his father's grave.

Rather than buy one, or cut and haul something to the graveyard, he removed an altar-table, marked it with his father's initials, and put it over the grave. He was subsequently fined £200 and sent to prison for his act.

Three kilometres from St Michael Penkevil, along wooded tracks punctuated with magnificent views of the Fal, lies the occasionally-used church at Lamorran.

It is so much a set-piece representation of a traditional riverside church that those passing by it – and it deserves a halt rather than a drive past – might easily believe that it is a part of a film or television set.

Between the church door and the nearby river there is one of Cornwall's most beautiful stone crosses, rugged and aged monitor of perhaps 500 years of worship. The tranquility is enhanced by soft blossom and by the bellhouse that stands apart from the church itself.

Ruan Church.

Ruan Lanihorne is said to have been built from the ruins of the castle that stood nearby when Ruan Lanihorne was an active and important river port. Certainly the tower dates back some six hundred years.

The font, like the altar-table, the alms boxes and the lectern support have been worked from ancient timbers removed from the original roof.

There was a strict segregation of those attending worship, the lords entering by the north door, the rector from the south, and the congregation by a door under the tower.

One of its most interesting wall-tablets is that recalling that a Mrs Ann Luke 'hath given in trust forever the interest of two hundred pounds with the pious Design of promoting religious Education of the poor Children of this Parish on condition of their keeping in repair a certain Tomb.'

Perhaps it is fortunate that education is now taken care of by the State, since the interest was on a sum 'vested in the 3 per cent Consols', and which probably no longer exists.

Arthur Mee says of Creed: 'The traveller should seek its church porch, for he will much enjoy its roof. The porch has been here 400 years, with triple shafts each side of its doorway, and the roof is a study in unusual carvings.' He also mentions 'some of the best medieval stone windows in Cornwall.'

All very true, indeed. But to the casual visitor who is interested in spectacle rather than architecture, Creed is well worth the detour just outside Tregony and which leads through an initially unpromising lane away from the main road.

It possesses one of the best-tended floral displays of exotic plants to be found in the locality, with spring-time bringing a clash between the aggressive brightness of thrusting daffodil, narcissus and other flowers, with the subdued suspended pastel-hue of azalea and rhododendron.

Saint Cuby is the patron saint of Tregony parish church.

Never heard of him?

Tregony Church.

The rugged stone cross at Lamorran churchyard.

Well, he was a local saint made good, having been born in Cornwall some 1,500 years ago. He was, it would seem, well-heeled and well-placed, being the son of Cornwall's first Christian king, Selyf, and the grandson of one of King Arthur's henchmen, Gereint.

Having been educated in Cornwall and France, Cuby made the obligatory trip to Jerusalem and returned with new convictions and a team of disciples. Renouncing all claim to the throne of Cornwall, he decided to become a missionary and established a Christian group at Tregony as well as one near Looe before setting off for Wales and Ireland, thereby reversing the traditional flow of missionaries into Cornwall from those nations.

Almost certainly the present church at Tregony, although much more modern, stands where St Cuby established his first settlement and links back to those days in a proud line of continuous Christian activity and worship.

It seems that the modern church has traces of Norman building, and with the squat and compact tower having been erected in the 1300s.

Most of the updating to its current appearance was carried out in the two major reconstructions of 1828 and 1899, the earlier of the two being designed to multiply the free sittings in the church virtually tenfold from 30 to 290. This was achieved by extending the eastern end of the church by almost two metres and by 'thinning' the thick walls to north and south. More significantly, though, the roof was redesigned and reconstructed to a single span of low pitch.

Sadly, it turned out to be a wrong choice in terms of mechanics! Gradually the unbalanced weight of roof versus walls began to tell and the south wall achieved so ominous an outwards bulge that it seemed it might explode assunder. As the architect called to look at the problem recorded, 'the dreadful havoc made to the fabric in 1828', made it necessary to restore the roof to its original two spans and to dismantle the large gallery put up at the west end sixty years earlier.

Silas Hocking must be the hero of any aspiring writer.

He is reputed to have been the first man ever to sell a million copies of his books during his lifetime and, like his brother, Joseph, was a prolific writer with a multitude of loyal and committed readers.

Silas and Joseph, and their parents, James and Elizabeth, are recalled in the cemetery of St Stephen-in-Brannel, over which there towers a functional, but dignified, pinnacled focal-point of the church and which has stood for more than 500 years.

The large church, built of rugged Cornish granite, has long-replaced the original Norman place of worship but which is still in evidence in the form of its font resplendent with carved trees and horrendous figures, like dragons, designed to scare evil away.

John Wesley visited St Stephen in 1757, recording on Sunday 25 September that: 'at two I preached in St Stephen's near a lone house on the side of a barren mountain; but neither the house nor the court could contain the people; so we went into a meadow where all might kneel (as they generally do in Cornwall) as well as stand and hear. And they did hear, and sing, and pray as for life. I saw none careless or inattentive among them.'

But of all the churches of the Fal, two must stand out both in their story and in their sheer beauty. They are Old Kea and the Quaker meeting house at Come-to-Good.

St Stephen-in-Brannel Church – dignified and towered.

St Kea is another saint with a wonderful story.

Known variously as Kea, Che, Landegea or the Chinese-sounding Lan-te-Ke, he arrived from Ireland at roughly the same time that Cuby was hot-footing it in the other direction.

Kea, it is said, was so unhappy to be left behind when his brother monks set off to help Christianise England that he prayed in his distress with such fervour that he passed into a swoon and awoke to find himself safely on a drifting boulder floating across the Irish Sea. Defying storm, tempest – and currents – the stone and St Kea were washed up at Churchtown Creek where, in the time-honoured fashion of saved or salvaged saints, he built a small monastery. He met two other saints, Fili who went to Philleigh, and Rumon, who went to Ruan Lanihorne.

Certainly Kea's monastery and influence flourished. The original parish of St Kea covered some 7,000 acres, including Kenwyn, Chacewater, Baldhu and Scorrier. A large church was needed. It was built, although little is known of its exact nature and design other than can be gathered from the ruined tower that is the sole survivor and which dates back to the fifteenth century.

Almost certainly it was dismantled by parishioners in 1802 when a new parish church, more centrally placed, was built several miles away. Some of the 'parts' went to other Cornish churches then being built. The bells were moved to the new parish church and, possibly at the urging and part-financing of Lord Falmouth, the tower was allowed to remain standing as it provided a dramatic feature of the view from Tregothnan.

It is recorded that some of the materials were used to provide a parish alms-house on the site, and that the alms-house itself then gave way to a little mission house erected in 1853, for the sum of £111.8s.0d. (£111.40p). For a time it was used, in addition to worship, as a local school and as a Sunday school.

In 1967 electric heating and lighting were installed and, sixteen years later, the fabric was brought up to date when the roof was re-slated, the windows repaired and the interior redecorated to add to the charm and atmosphere of the Fal's 'doll's house' church.

If Old Kea has a natural charm, then it is equalled by that of the Quaker meeting house at Come-to-Good.

However appropriate 'Come-to-Good' might seem for a house of prayer, the name actually comes from the Cornish 'Cwm-ty-quite' meaning, equally aptly and romantically, 'combe in the woods'.

The ruined tower of Old Kea Church.

Creed Church – 'well worth a detour'.

In the late 1600s, Cornwall's Quakers faced repression and imprisonment merely because they were believed to be speaking against the theology and interests of the established church.

One of them, Grace Burgess, was incarcerated in Launceston gaol for no other reason than that she had spoken in private at a Quaker meeting. Another woman, Susannah Daniell, suffered the same fate. A third, Dorothy Waugh, was locked up for two weeks merely because she attended a meeting.

The Truro Quakers were hounded out of their meeting place by constables and driven through the streets with violence and abuse.

In Falmouth, too, the Quakers became a threatened society. In 1657, according to records: 'the soldiers being sent from Pendennis Castle, hindered us from the quiet holding thereof but we met noe violent persecution until the return of King Charles Steward in 1660, and we were then most of us taken up and imprisoned and although some fell in that trying day yet most of friends outlived that exercise and tryalls of many reproaches and threatenings of punishment and loss of goods which was often our portion.'

Restrictions on the Quakers increased.

In an attempt to stamp them out, laws were introduced that made it illegal for more than five people to meet for any form of worship

Old Kea – 'the doll's house church'.

The meeting house at Come-to-Good.

other than that ordered by the Prayer Book; it became an offence to speak at a prayer meeting or a gathering, or to permit or encourage the holding of a meeting or a gathering. On top of that there was a fine of one shilling – 5p – for not attending public worship at the parish church.

Holding weddings and funerals became liable to imprisonment or fine. Opinions hardened, and then moderated against the Quakers. One of Truro's parish constables admitted on his death bed that 'what I have done against the Quakers is the greatest sin I have committed in all my life.'

The Toleration Act, of 1689, paved the way to less harsh times. But, by then, the Quakers were well on the way to establishing their refuge at Come-to-Good in what is now the oldest Quaker meeting house in England.

Dating back to 1710, it is one of only three such thatched, buttressed, clay and straw buildings in the country.

It is as if time has stood still there, isolated from the outside world by an invisible curtain of absolute peace, warmth and love.

The day of the first meeting is described as being 'a rainy one and an abundance of people were out that could not get in and some went away again. It was our new house and first meeting in it.'

Congregations grew and some of as many as 1,000 friends were recorded, with overflow meetings being held outside and addressed by speakers on horseback.

Perhaps the finest description of Come-to-Good meeting house and its grounds is that of L Violet Hodgkin: 'The small old white meeting house is surrounded by a yet older small green burial-ground where long grasses and flowers innumerable cover the gentle slopes. The soft mounds cluster round the walls; as if those who were laid there had wished that their bodies might rest as near as possible to the house of peace where their spirits had rested while on earth.'

Mylor Church porch in 1921.

If there truly is a crock of gold where the rainbow ends, then the rainbow that touches Come-to-Good kisses a wealth of peace and faith that cannot be bought with earthly riches.

The oldest saint recognised by the churches of the Fal is Melorus who gave his name to Mylor and where he was martyred, where the church now stands, in 411.

Despite the violence of his death, Mylor church and churchyard – like Come-to-Good – radiates warmth, charm and beauty.

Dating back to 1308, the church boasts two Norman doorways as well as a magnificent 15th century entrance to the south porch.

Beside the entrance stands the largest round-headed cross ever to have been found in Cornwall, more than three metres high. It may even have marked St Melorus' grave but, for some unexplained reason, was only found in the 19th century when, upside down, it was discovered acting as a prop to help hold up the south wall of the church in 1870.

St Melorus' cross, Mylor.

The churchyard is rich in old gravestones and fascinating epitaphs which spell out a social history. They include a man shot by Customs officers; the famous vicar, Thomas Peters, who lived in the days of Cromwell and who went to America to become first minister at the settlement of New London before returning to complete his incumbency; and victims of shipwreck and drowning.

Among them are those who perished in the disaster in which death claimed almost two hundred souls from the transport *Queen*, wrecked off Trefusis in January 1814 in 'a scene of indescribable horror and confusion' when those standing helpless on the shore could hear 'the alarming shrieks of the women and children, whom neither force nor entreaty could render quiet' until, with fallen masts and shattered timbers, she totally disintegrated.

Indeed, the rapidly-rising number of victims of the sea being buried at Mylor created a horrendous state of overcrowded and privileged affairs in the churchyard where the wealthy were buried in drained land and the poor in swamp, leading to a report that: 'the drained part is reserved for those who entertain the idea that even in death they will be somewhat better than their poorer neighbours, and that the undrained portion falls to the lot of those who have had but little of this world's goods.'

In 1871 an army pensioner 'deserving of the highest honour' was buried in a grave awash with water while the dead wife of a Royal Marine was laid to rest with a man dipping water out of the grave while the burial service was actually being read.

But in this immortal account of the death of Joseph Grapp, who died in 1770, Mylor churchyard surely has the most succinct epitaph of all time:

Alass, Friend Joseph,
His end wear Almost Sudden,
As thou the mandate came
Express from Heaven.
His foot it slip, and he did fall,
Help, help, he cries, and that was all.

To the
Memory of the
WARRIORS,
Women and Children,
who on their return to England
from the Coast of Spain;
unhappily perished
in the Wreck of the
Queen Transport,
on Trefusis Point Jan.y 14. 1814
This Stone is erected as a Testimony
of regret for their fate by the
Inhabitants of this Parish

Warrior memorial, Mylor.

88

OYSTERS, CLAY, BOATS AND PLUMS
The industries of the Fal

BOATBUILDERS and boatmen, seamen and smugglers, fishermen and fruit-growers and clay-workers ... all have their place in the history of the Fal.

Times and techniques have changed, but many of the old activities exist as much today as they have for centuries although, admittedly in rather more technicalised guise and resorting, arguably, to brain-power rather than to mere brawn.

One of the earliest recorded occupations is that connected with the wool trade in the thirteenth century when the townspeople of Grampound worked the mills of the old manor of Tybesta for John of

Falmouth quay punts taking part in a regatta in 1895.

Cornish sheep – 'small bodies with little wool.'

Eltham, who had granted them their charter. Paying royalties to the lord of the manor for the use of his water, the mill-workers would carry out the final rites of the manufacture of woollen cloth, dipping it into water and then pounding its texture into flexibility with the use of heavy hammers or stones.

Certainly a tough treatment was necessary for Cornish sheep had small bodies with little wool. What was produced was of a very rough quality and, whilst the industry of Dartmoor and Devon had become one of the Westcountry's first major exports, the products of Cornwall stayed very much to the west of the Tamar to provide clothing for the Cornish themselves.

But, ignoring the importance of traditional minerals, it was St Stephen-in-Brannel that was, in the mid-1700s, to lead to the establishment of one of Cornwall's most important and most successful industries – china clay.

Having hunted Cornwall for something similar to the clay used in Chinese porcelain, William Cookworthy found major deposits near St Stephen. He took many years of patient research to discover how best to use the mineral but, by experiment and, eventually, by raising the firing temperature beyond what had ever been used before, he produced the first real porcelain to be made in the United Kingdom, taking out a patent in 1768, and starting production in Plymouth.

Working to Cookworthy's patent and direction, the famous Staffordshire potteries, Minton, Wedgwood and Spode, took over the actual production of porcelain and influenced the development of china clay recovery in Cornwall, working the pits near St Austell, and shipping out to the potteries through Charlestown.

Although there was a great demand for porcelain products, the growth of the industry was slow. In 1814 there were less than ten pits being worked near St Stephen, with an average output of only two hundred tons apiece per annum, as against a current figure measured in millions of tons and now representing almost a quarter of the total production of the whole world.

Cookworthy probably had little idea of the potential of what he had discovered when, having looked at possible deposits at Tregonning Hill, near Helston, he went to St Stephen and found: 'that in the neighbourhood of the parish of St Stephens, in Cornwall, there are immense quantities of both the petunste stone & the caulin (kaolin), and which I believe may be more commodiously and advantageously wrought than do those at Tregonnin Hill ... they

An old photograph of workers bagging clay in 1895.

91

New mobility for Cornwall in 1900 with the advent of the motor car. These early motorists were having a look at the deep clay pits near St Austell.

produce a much whiter body, and do not shrink so much by far in baking, nor take stains so readily from the fire . . . The parish of Dennis, the next to St Stephens, I believe, hath both the ingredients in plenty in it. I know of two quarries of the stone – one is just above St Stephens, the other is called Caluggas.'

Looking at the deposits, and reasoning that the poverty of Cornwall and the ignorance of the people as to the uses of the clay 'were so plentiful in the county and in the hands of so many landowners, they could not expect any high rent for them', Cookworthy reckoned that low rents would cushion the cost of transport which, in any case, would already be subsidised by farmers willing to take china clay to the ports in carts that would otherwise have been empty on their way to collect incoming lime and sea-sand.

He thought that it would be less costly to send the clay away to the Staffordshire potteries than to set up potteries in Cornwall as it was cheaper to transport light-weight china clay than to ship heavy coal.

Having settled his basic business plan, he was somewhat surprised when, having offered his first land-owner a rent of ten guineas (£10.50) a year just for access to the clay, he was asked for double that figure.

Cookworthy stuck out, the deal was sealed and working the deposits began in 1779.

He was delighted. Not only had he secured his first source, but other landowners were happy to turn a useless material into cash with no risk involved. He had, as he told a business colleague, 'plenty of good growan clay to offer it to all the world at – say – four shillings (20p) a ton mine rent . . . and the expense of raising it is a trifle.'

Despite its comparatively slow and cautious start, the china clay industry prospered and grew around St Stephen although not without its share of industrial problems and occasional industrial sabotage.

In September 1877, one forward-looking company tried the system, used in California, of using high-pressure jets of water to wash minerals from their surrounds rather than merely to excavate manually.

Clayworkers, fearing that any new mechanisation might imperil their jobs, entered the pit overnight and slashed and cut the hoses to such an extent as to render them totally useless. A report on the incident commented on the strange fact, suggesting an organised 'inside job', that: 'the windows do not appear to have been tampered

The car followed the clay – 1900.

Bal maidens in long sleeved frocks and starched bonnets in 1905.

with, and those who perpetrated the outrage seem to have had free access. It is supposed that prejudice must be at the root of this matter – machinery being looked upon as a way of getting rid of men. In this case the machinery is intended to more perfectly do what is now done by men, and it is a process accompanied by far less inconvenience to the men than the one now in use.'

Feock, hardly regarded nowadays as a centre of industry, boasted a lead smelting works in the 1830s and capable of turning out one hundred and eighty tons of lead each month. The works, at Penpol, were set on a quay with the useful bonus capability of connecting with the Redruth railway and access to the tin mines for timber and coal inwards and ore as a return cargo.

Half a century on, however, the story was one of constant contraction rather than of growth. The great Perran foundry complex, including a saw-mill at Devoran; the Norway Inn; river frontages; timber storage; stables; storehouses; stockyards; machinery and warehouses was up for sale. The auctioneer's advertisement, in November 1880, described just part of the former holding as 'the premises where Colan and James Harvey almost "coined" money in the timber and other trades 25 years ago. £50,000 a year is said to have been their lowest turn over during the time they held this.'

A young woman bends down to dip a jug in the creek at Kea early this century.

At Feock Downs, near Come-to-Good, they had made the finest ropes for mines and ships, the rural air pungent with the unusually heady smell of hemp and pitchblend, with barns and cow-sheds jockeying for prominence with rope-houses and hemp-lofts, furnaces and capstans.

Grampound already had its still-to-be-found oak-bark tannery where oak bark was fashioned and prepared for uses totally beyond the flexibility of even the finest of leathers.

Then there was the boat-building along the banks of the Fal. Craft of beautiful lines, many built under almost primitive conditions in yards that consisted of a few huts on the riverside and a couple of saw-pits in which the vessel was actually constructed. Wood was obtained from the cheapest source – either from the nearest woodlands, or else as off-cuts or 'surplus' from the larger yards. Work-forces were small and usually came from one family, each member carefully selected, instructed and initiated to maintain the greatest skills between the least number of craftsmen. It was all done with an eye on the job. Drawings, models, templates, designs were virtually unknown and the craft grew as an amalgam of craftsmen's 'feel' and progressive development.

When a yard won a commission, the first task was to dig a saw-pit

Grampound oak bark tannery in 1989.

The oyster beds off Tolverne were virtually worked out.

Kea's plum gardens in 1887.

in the most convenient place. Secondly, the keel-blocks were set up. Then, as the timber arrived, local carpenters would cut out the ribs, the frames and the planks, passing them to the shipwrights who would assemble the ship at the waterside.

Despite their almost casual construction, boats built on the Fal had a world-wide reputation for stamina and seaworthiness and lasted as much as twice or even four times as long as they were designed to do.

Occasionally there was a milestone – such as March 1875 when 'a large concourse of people' gathered at Stephens' yard at Devoran to see the launching of the first schooner ever built there. Constructed for a Welsh owner, she was – with a displacement of two hundred and forty tons – the largest vessel ever built up-river from Restronguet.

Many of the ships built on the Fal worked the river throughout their lives, either in the oyster fishery; in connection with deep-water ships laid-up at King Harry ferry; or used by one or other of generations of Truro River pilots who navigated deeper-draught ships between Truro and Carrick Roads with a mixture of knowledge, seamanship and memory.

With the banks sometimes obscured by fog, or in pitch darkness, the pilots gave the ships in their charge safe passage in a waterway devoid of formal navigation-lights. They knew the lights of farm-houses and cottages, and lined-up on them. They knew the sounds from a milking shed and took their bearings from them. They knew that an almost undetectable breeze meant a junction between main river and a creek or inlet.

Indeed, when the Royal Yacht *Britannia* visited Falmouth in 1977, and Her Majesty had been inundated with Cornish pasties from well-wishers wherever she had gone on her Cornish Silver Jubilee tour, the

Overleaf, the New Resolute passenger boat packed with a cargo of pleasure seekers.

Queen was told of one pilot who, it was said, was so familiar with the ingredients and the hunger-inducing odour of pasties cooked in each farmhouse and cottage near the river that he could identify his exact position by cross-sniffing.

But, as Her Majesty put it: 'That sounds very much like an old Cornish pilot's wife's tale.'

From the 1850s the Fal, 'The English Rhine' as it was advertised in holiday brochures, took on a new and growing form of river traffic in the form of passenger boats. Sleek, elegant and dignified they were initially the exclusive pleasure of the well-heeled. But, by 1888 when *New Resolute* joined the growing fleet, the fares were at such a level that a much wider range of travellers could enjoy the peace and beauty of the river as well as, in some cases, using the boats as a welcome alternative to road transport to get to work.

It was, and to a lesser degree, still is, a wonderful and restful sight to see the registered oyster fishermen carefully and lovingly harvesting their catch under controlled conditions requiring the immediate return to the beds of any immature stock. Dredges, rather like net shopping-bags held open with a wire frame, are dragged gently

Fal oyster boat off the Pandora Inn in 1895.

100

A woodcutter at Kea splits timber at the turn of the century.

along the bed . . . coaxing, teasing, snaring, lifting and then tipping for hand-sorting on the deck of the oyster boat.

Almost a century ago, in October 1897, at the start of the oyster season, over one hundred dredgers began work at the same time. In the first two days over three quarters of a million oysters were taken, in total reversal of the fears at the end of the previous season that the beds off Tolverne were virtually worked out.

The oysters, it was said, looked very well, were very plentiful and gave promise of a good season.

From the harvest of the sea to the harvest of the fruit . . . and the excellence of that little oasis of plum orchards around Coombe or Cowland Creek where the adventurous could row their boats right up under the trees and shake them off over-burdened boughs.

Once more the files of *The West Briton* paint a tranquil but magical display of words: 'In the spring, when clothed with their wealth of snowy blossom, these orchards present a very beautiful appearance when viewed either from the water or the surrounding hills. In August the harvest commences, and in September it is in full swing; then busy hands are at work in every orchard, vehicles of all descriptions come and go, steamers bring their passengers, and pedestrians from many miles around pay their yearly visit to the "plum gardens". The work of shaking and picking begins at eight a.m. and

101

ends at five p.m., with an interval of an hour allowed for dinner, yet that of sorting and counting, which is carried on indoors, may proceed for two, three or even more hours longer. The method of counting is by 'casts' of five, twenty-one casts constitute one hundred of plums. The baskets used are lined with fern, or perhaps a little dry grass, but never with straw, as a musty odour proceeds from it which would spoil the flavour of the fruit. When a basket is packed a layer of fern is placed on the top and secured by wooden spears very similar to those used by thatchers; these are laid across the top, the ends being sharpened and driven through the sides of the baskets.'

The harvest of fish, the harvest of fruit, but what of that most exciting harvest of all . . . the harvest of contraband, the harvest of smuggling?

With its many coves, inlets, hamlets and beaches the Fal must have been a smugglers' paradise. Yet while suspicion and romance point to the probability of illicit imports, the factual records are silent – other than with two fascinating clues.

In 1840, in Tregony, a mob assembled with bundles of reeds and faggots of wood in order to burn the effigy of a woman who, it was believed, had given information to the authorities against a local man discovered with a keg of contraband spirits in his possession.

But, more significantly, it is worth looking at the Rules and Orders of the Grampound Amicable Society, a charitable body formed in 1772 to assist the sick and disabled of the locality.

Bearing in mind that it is a tradition of insurance companies to debar or discourage those who might most likely qualify for benefit, it almost passes without comment that the Society had decided that, in addition to those incapacitated by venereal disease, or those injured through fighting or wrestling, nobody injured whilst engaged in smuggling should be covered by welfare payments.

The upper reaches of the River Fal at Tregony.

Acknowledgements

In his search for illustrations, the author wishes to extend and record his grateful thanks to: Peter Gilson, Royal Cornwall Polytechnic Society, Falmouth; Peter Hawkins and Susan Dallow, Wheal Martyn China Clay Museum, Carthew, St Austell; Stewart and Sylvia Hood; Roger Penhallurick, Royal Institution of Cornwall, Truro; and the National Trust. He thanks his wife, Diana, for her many modern photographs and is furious that her interpretations and compositions always turn out better than his own.

Books consulted

Barratt, Rex	*Stately Homes in and around Truro*	Dyllanslow Truran
Baring-Gould, S	*Cornish Characters and Strange Events*	The Bodley Head
Barton, D Bradford	*Life in Cornwall in the 19th Century*	Barton
Barton, R M	*A History of the Cornish China Clay Industry*	Barton
Berry, Claude	*A Portrait of Cornwall*	Robert Hale
Bird, Sheila	*Around the Waterways of the Fal*	Bird of Paradise
Brown, H Miles	*The Church in Cornwall*	Blackford
Calamy, Edmund	*Account of the Ejected Ministers*	–
	Chambers Biographical Dictionary	Chambers
Davey, Cyril	*A Cornish Holiday*	Epworth House
Davidson, Robin	*Cornwall*	Batsford
	Dictionary of National Biography	Oxford University Press
Douch, H L	*Old Cornish Inns*	Barton
Fiennes, Celia	*Diaries and Travels*	
Fox, Barclay	*Barclay Fox's Journal*	Hyman and Bell
Gardner, John	*Coastal Sailing Craft*	Hugh Evelyn
Gilbert, Davies	*Parochial History of Cornwall*	J B Nichols & Son
Halliday, F E	*A History of Cornwall*	Duckworth
Henderson, Charles	*Essays in Cornish History*	Barton
Lake, William	*A Complete Parochial History of the County of Cornwall*	Lake
Laws, Peter	*A Guide to the National Trust in Devon and Cornwall*	David & Charles
Mee, Arthur	*Cornwall*	Hodder & Stoughton
Norden, John	*Description of Cornwall*	Frank Graham
Oliver, Hugh	*A History of the Parish of Mylor*	Barnicott & Pearce
Pearce, John	*The Wesleys in Cornwall*	Barton
Pearse, Richard	*The Ports and Harbours of Cornwall*	H E Warne
Pesvner, Niklaus	*The Buildings of England*	Penguin
Pettitt, Paul	*New Shell Guide of Devon & Cornwall*	Michael Joseph
Pope, Dudley	*At 12 Mr Byng Was Shot*	Weidenfeld & Nicolson
Quixley, R C E	*Antique Maps of Cornwall and the Isles of Scilly*	Quixley
Rolt, L T C	*The Cornish Giant*	Lutterworth
Speed, John	*John Speed's England*	Phoenix House
Stockdale, F W L	*Excursions through Cornwall 1824*	Barton
Stubbs, Jean	*Great Houses of Cornwall*	Bossiney Books
Synge, Patrick M	*The Gardens of Britain (Devon and Cornwall)*	Batsford
Ward Lock & Co	*Falmouth Guides*	Ward Lock & Co

Files of *The West Briton* and *The Royal Cornwall Gazette*, and various church and parish guides.

ALSO AVAILABLE:

AROUND ST AUSTELL BAY
by Joy Wilson
An exploration in words and old photographs around one of the most beautiful bays in Britain.
'... Joy Wilson's text is as warm and as sympathetic as the lovely old pictures, making this a book which glows with interest, a soft lamplight shedding illumination on an era dimmed by the passing years. It is a beautiful achievement ...'
The Western Morning News

GREAT HOUSES OF CORNWALL
by Jean Stubbs
The well-known novelist tours seven National Trust properties.
'... she finds a rich vein of history and human interest ...'
The Cornish Guardian

100 YEARS AROUND THE LIZARD
by Jean Stubbs
A beautiful title, relating to a magical region of Cornwall, well illustrated, with text by the distinguished novelist living near Helston.
'... the true flavour of life on the windswept peninsula, past and present ... the strange qualities of the flat landscape, the effects of the elements on people's daily lives and, above all, the contrast of past and present are distilled in the text.'
Cornish Life

SEA STORIES OF CORNWALL
by Ken Duxbury, 48 photographs
'This is a tapestry of true tales', writes the author, 'by no means all of them disasters – which portray something of the spirit, the humour, the tragedy, and the enchantment, that is the lot of we who know the sea.'
'... a good mixture of stories, well told by a man with a close affinity to the sea and ships.'
Geoffrey Underwood
Western Evening Herald

FOWEY – RIVER AND TOWN
by Sarah Foot
An enlarged and updated edition of Following the River Fowey.
'The intricate tapestries of this delightful area is woven together with warm, understanding interviews ... buy, beg or borrow it.'
The Cornish Times

DAPHNE du MAURIER COUNTRY
by Martyn Shallcross
A very special look at Cornwall in that the internationally-famous novelist has set important stories here. Explores locations which fired Dame Daphne's imagination. The subject of a Radio Cornwall series, produced by Tamsin Mitchell.
'... Anyone whose appreciation of the beauty of Cornwall has been enhanced by Dame Daphne's writing will enjoy this book – a fitting tribute to a remarkable lady.'
Cornish Life

MY CORNWALL
A personal vision of Cornwall by eleven writers who lived and worked in the county: Daphne du Maurier, Ronald Duncan, James Turner, Angela du Maurier, Jack Clemo, Denys Val Baker, Colin Wilson, C. C. Vyvyan, Arthur Caddick, Michael Williams and Derek Tangye with reproductions of paintings by Margo Maeckelberghe.
'An ambitious collection of chapters.'
The Times, London

AROUND & ABOUT THE ROSELAND
by David Mudd
David Mudd explores the Roseland and brings to life much of its exciting past.

UNKNOWN CORNWALL
by Michael Williams
84 drawings and photographs nearly all especially commissioned for this publication, portraying features of Cornwall rarely seen on the published page.
'... a treasure chest of rich jewels that will surprise many people who pride themselves on a thorough knowledge ...'
Western Evening Herald

WESTCOUNTRY MYSTERIES
introduced by Colin Wilson
A team of authors probe mysterious happenings in Somerset, Devon and Cornwall.
Drawings and photographs all add to the mysterious content.
'A team of authors have joined forces to re-examine and probe various yarns from the puzzling to the tragic.'
James Belsey, Bristol Evening Post

THE CRUEL CORNISH SEA
by David Mudd
Cornish shipwrecks spanning 400 years.

COASTLINE OF CORNWALL
by Ken Duxbury
Ken Duxbury has spent thirty years sailing the seas of Cornwall, walking its clifftops, exploring its caves and beaches, using its harbour and creeks. Over 100 photographs, 45 in colour.
'... a trip in words and pictures from Hawker's Morwenstow in the north, round Land's End and the Lizard to the gentle slopes of Mount Edgcumbe country park.'
The Western Morning News

We shall be pleased to send you our catalogue giving full details of our growing list of titles for Devon, Cornwall, Somerset, Dorset and Wiltshire as well as forthcoming publications. If you have difficulty in obtaining our titles, write direct to Bossiney Books, Land's End, St Teath, Bodmin, Cornwall.